Writing Philosophy Papers

Zachary Seech

Palomar College

Wadsworth Publishing Company
Belmont, California
A Division of Wadsworth, Inc.

Philosophy Editor: *Kenneth King*

Editorial Assistant: *Gay Meixel*

Production: *Ruth Cottrell*

Print Buyer: *Randy Hurst*

Cover and Interior Design: *Michael Rogondino*

Copy Editor: *Ruth Cottrell*

Cover Photograph: © *Stuart Simons, 1990*

Signing Representative: *Howard Perry*

Compositor: *Scratchgravel Publishing Services*

Printer: *Malloy Lithographing, Inc.*

Printed in the United States of America

3 4 5 6 7 8 9 10—97 96 95 94

Library of Congress Cataloguing-in-Publication Data

Seech, Zachary.
  Writing philosophy papers / Zachary Seech.
    p.   cm.
  Includes bibliographical references and index.
  ISBN 0-534-19758-2
  1. Philosophy—Authorship.   2. Philosophy—Study and teaching.
  I. Title.
  B52.7.S44   1992
  808'.0661—dc20   92-35465
                                                      CIP

To my parents
Ann and Elmer Seech

Contents

Preface

Writing Philosophy Papers goes beyond general instructions on paper writing. The whole book focuses on how to write *philosophy* papers. The five kinds of papers most often assigned in philosophy classes are explained, and a whole chapter is devoted to writing the traditional philosophy paper: the thesis defense paper. Chapter 7 explains how to use specific philosophical resources.

Whether it's a question about organization, documentation, research, or writing style, the student will now have the answer *before* the paper is submitted to the professor. This should be a relief both to the professor who reads and grades the papers and to the student who can hardly do a good job of writing a paper if the task itself is unclear.

Professors assign different types of papers. *Writing Philosophy Papers* shows students that many paper assignments are hybrids of the five basic kinds. The students learn the basic skills in these chapters despite varying instructions for their specific classroom assignments. Professors may also specify a preferred style of documentation. Footnotes and endnotes are illustrated in this book. So is the MLA parenthetical documentation. Both methods are clearly displayed in a sample paper. In-text citation and the number system of documentation are also explained.

The focus is on philosophy. The many examples throughout *Writing Philosophy Papers* are from philosophical concepts or primary and secondary sources in philosophy. In addition, there is a discussion of philosophy courses, philosophical topics, argumentation and fallacies, philosophy journals and resource books, as well as *The Philosopher's Index.*

* * * * * * * * * * *

I learned to write philosophy papers from many of my former professors and also, in various ways, from my students. There are too many people to name. Nevertheless, I thank them all. My colleagues have also been very helpful. I thank the members of the Behavioral Sciences Department at Palomar College for their consistent and sincere support. Michael Lockett in particular helped on this project. Bob Call of the Palomar College library was also helpful. I thank George Boggs, president of Palomar College, for his support of faculty authors. I also appreciate the cooperation of Professor Richard H. Lineback, director of the Philosophy Documentation Center at Bowling Green State University.

Ken King, philosophy editor at Wadsworth Publishing Company, who initiated the project, had the expertise to direct it professionally and the resolution to move it along remarkably efficiently. The book is better because of his concern for its success.

The book is also better because of Gay Meixel, Bob Kauser, and Ruth Cottrell. The prompt and insightful reviews of John L. King, University of North Carolina at Greensboro, and Scott C. Lowe, Bloomsburg University, were very helpful to me. Finally, I thank my wife, children, and parents their help and support.

Z. S.

Introduction

We call them "papers." In college, professors require students to write papers to show how well they think and research, and how well they understand and express ideas. These same professors write and publish papers of their own for the benefit of other professors and thinkers around the country.

People often toss around ideas, collecting a little information through newspapers or magazines, voicing their own opinions and criticizing other viewpoints. But rarely do we take the time to develop our thoughts fully on a single topic. Half-baked ideas are sometimes the only items on our daily menus.

Writing a paper is a good way to develop your ideas on one topic in a thorough and precise way. You make an effort to prethink and rethink your ideas. You reword those first, faulty phrases and express your best thoughts in the best way you can. You don't know how good you are until you've done it. The result should be something you can be proud of, something that displays clear thinking and good language skills. You end up with a physical product, a set of printed pages that shows your reflective judgment on an issue. The educational process often leaves nothing more tangible to testify to your skills.

Unfortunately, students sometimes lose this opportunity to express their ideas in an impressive way. The testimony of this loss comes in words of complaint and lament:

- The paper is due tomorrow and I haven't even started it yet.
- I have no idea what the professor wants for this paper.
- What is she going to grade on, anyway?
- I haven't obtained the books I need, and now it's too late.
- I'm on the last page of my paper, and now I see that I can't prove what I said I would in the first part of the paper. What can I do?
- What does he mean by argue for?

Much of what students need to know about writing a paper goes unsaid. There is so much for the student to know and so little time for the teacher to teach the basics of paper writing. *Writing Philosophy Papers* is written to help professors advise their students on how to write a philosophy paper and to give students in philosophy classes a better chance to demonstrate their skills. If you study this book carefully, one of the frequent obstacles to learning should be largely overcome. Good luck.

1

First Things First

You have been instructed to write a paper for a philosophy course. Here is your first advice:

Start right away.

Whether the paper is due this week, next month, or two months from now, do something about it today or tomorrow. Even if you can't start the heaviest phase of your work yet, getting the project going will ease your mind. It can also give you ideas to turn over in your mind and help you plan your time. Putting off the first steps often results in a late paper, a poorly written paper, or both.

How do you start? This depends on how well you understand the assignment, when it is due, and what the assignment is.

Know the Assignment

Sometimes it is difficult to do a job well even when you know exactly what must be done. Very seldom can you do a good job when someone else sets the goal and the goal isn't clear to you.

You can't expect to write the kind of paper your professor has in mind if you don't understand what the requirements are. If you were absent or late even once, find out whether you missed any oral or written instructions. If you missed written instructions, obtain a copy. If you missed oral instructions, copy them from a student who took good notes or ask the professor. Read the instructions carefully. Reread them. Study them. Ask your questions early.

Know the Criteria for Evaluation

Be sure you understand how your work will be evaluated and graded. Here is a list of common criteria for evaluating student papers in philosophy. Your professor may use some of these expressions in somewhat different ways, but the general explanation offered for each criterion will still be helpful.

- *Choice of topic or thesis:* Your topic or thesis should not be too broad to be covered thoroughly or too narrow to be worth covering. If you are defending a point of view, it should not be so uncontentious that hardly any reasonable person will disagree, or so far-fetched that no argument can make it seem plausible. (See Chapters 1 and 2.)

- *Tone:* Most assignments of college papers call for an objective tone, without inflammatory language or indignant tone. Even when you defend one view, do not sound closed-minded. (See Chapter 2.)

- *Strength of argumentation:* When arguing for a thesis or point of view, offer reasons that an unbiased, clear-thinking person would find persuasive. (See Chapter 2.)

- *Balance of presentation:* When presenting information or evidence, your position is usually strengthened rather than weakened when you discuss alternative views on the issue and explain why you think it is reasonable to favor one of them. However, this criterion varies, depending on the purpose of the paper. (See Chapter 2.)

- *Organization of paper:* The opening paragraph usually announces the task its author undertakes, and it often previews the main parts of the paper. The paper should have an appropriate closing paragraph, and all transitions should be clear and smooth. (See Chapters 2, 4, and 5.)

- *Accuracy:* When presenting information or explaining some-one else's views, be careful not to misrepresent. Careless wording can skew the ideas in subtle but important ways. (See Chapter 5.)

- *Use of language:* Correct grammar and spelling are expected. Punctuation should be used correctly. Avoid unnecessarily complicated or obscure phrases and sentences. Be precise, choosing your words carefully. Always edit and rewrite your papers. (See Chapter 5.)

- *Originality:* If there are academic sins, plagiarism is among the most damning. You plagiarize when you use another author's wording (or wording close to it) in a way that allows a reader to conclude that the words are yours. Ideas, not only wording, can be plagiarized. Always indicate the source of any information, thoughts, or wording that you have borrowed for use in your paper. (See Chapter 6.)

- *Format:* If a specific form for references, page set-up, and presentation of your paper is designated, follow that form. If your topic seems to justify a departure from the assigned format, consult the professor before writing the paper. (See Chapter 6.)

- *Research:* Use credible sources as you put your paper together. Use enough research information to justify your claims. Your research should be thorough and relevant to your topic. (See Chapter 7.)

- *Neatness:* Papers should be clean, with few if any handwritten edits on a typed or computer-printed paper. Typing or computer preparation may be required. If the paper is handwritten, it must be able to be read easily and have no scratched out words.

These criteria may vary in importance, depending on the professor and the assignment. In some cases, a glaring weakness in only one of these categories will be enough to drop your overall grade below passing. For example, if your grammar or the strength of your argumentation is very poor, you may not receive a passing grade, no matter how well you accomplish some of the other tasks.

Schedule Your Time

After you are sure you understand the assignment and how it will be evaluated, you should break the project down into specific tasks and set a deadline for each of them. This will enable you to work at an effective pace.

As you write out your schedule, take into consideration your other school and nonschool obligations, the availability of resources like computers and hard-to-get books, and the due dates of the paper and any preliminary submissions you are required to make. Don't schedule your tasks so tightly that unforeseen personal emergencies will prevent you from completing the paper on time.

Try scheduling *backward* from the final due date (and any fixed dates for an outline, a rough draft, or other work that must be submitted). Ask yourself how many days you probably need —not the minimum you need if all goes well—to type, edit, and proofread a final copy. Write a target date on your schedule. Now continue scheduling backward. Write dates for the following sorts of things: your final rough draft; a first complete draft; a first draft of each major part of the paper; a revised outline; completion of library research; preparation of a first outline; topic selection. When you are done you may find that you do not have as much time as you want. There is usually no choice except to go back to your schedule and compress it. Even when you are working under strict time constraints, some peace of mind comes from knowing you have a schedule that will allow you to write the paper on time.

Some of your tasks can be delayed by circumstances beyond your control. Get to those things early. You can apply at your local library for interlibrary loans for books from other libraries, but the books may take weeks to arrive. Scheduled interviews are sometimes cancelled. Computers to which other people have access are sometimes unavailable when you need them. Finally, some books and articles yield slow reading, and some kinds of research are time-consuming.

Here is a sample of a short schedule. The dates indicate when each part of the project should be completed.

Feb. 4:	Topic selection
Feb. 24:	Outline

| Mar. 8: | Rough draft |
| Mar. 18: | Final copy |

You can also plan your intended workdays and the tasks for each day. Here is a sample of a more detailed schedule.

Feb. 2:	Spend day in library checking on topics
Feb. 4:	Select topic
Feb. 5:	Look for resources; apply for interlibrary loans
Feb. 7–13:	No time to work on paper this week!
Feb. 14:	Do research, 2–4 PM
Feb. 16–21:	Do research & write outline
Feb. 24:	Revise outline & write
Feb. 28:	Write
Mar. 5–8:	Write & revise
Mar. 8:	Finish rough draft
Mar. 11, 13:	Revise
Mar. 14, 15:	Enter paper in computer
Mar. 16:	Review & revise
Mar. 18:	Enter revision and print final copy

Post your neatly written, typed, or computer-printed schedule where you will see it every day. As the days or weeks pass, record the *actual* completion date for that task in the margin next to each item. If you fall behind by more than a few days, you may have to revise your schedule.

Types of Philosophy Papers

Thesis defense papers are assigned very often in philosophy classes. The purpose of a thesis defense paper is to state a position and give reasons for believing it is true. For example, you might, on an issue in ethics, claim that "Major corporations have a moral obligation to repair the environmental damage they have done." Reliable evidence and strong reasoning are at the heart of a good thesis defense paper. Chapter 2 is all about thesis defense papers.

Other kinds of papers are sometimes assigned. The purpose of **compare and contrast papers** is to show how two views, books, or philosophies are alike and how they differ. The purpose of **analysis papers** is to identify and examine some elements or aspects of a concept, book, article, or a philosopher's system of thought. The purpose of **research papers** is to survey important views that have been published on a certain topic. The purpose of **summary papers** is to restate someone else's views in your own words. These kinds of papers, and some hybrids of them, are discussed in Chapter 3.

Philosophy Courses and Sample Paper Topics

Most Introduction to Philosophy courses provide some instruction in ethics, metaphysics, and epistemology. Sometimes political philosophy and philosophy of religion are included in the introductory course. For your paper, you should probably choose a topic that relates to material that has been presented in the class. Get the professor's approval before working on a topic that relates only indirectly to course readings and lectures. In some cases, the professor will assign a topic or hand out a list of acceptable topics.

Most other philosophy courses focus on one area within philosophy. Here are descriptions of several areas of philosophy and some sample paper topics for courses in these areas. (These topic phrases may serve as titles of papers. They are not theses. A thesis is stated in sentence form.)

- *Ethics: The study of moral rights and responsibilities.* Sample topics: Why corporations have moral obligations; A morally justifiable national policy on abortion; A utilitarian justification of affirmative action; Who is responsible to care for AIDS patients?; Two views of Kant's moral imperative.

- *Political philosophy: The study of political rights and obligations; the study of social justice.* Sample topics: What should a person do when conscience conflicts with law?; Martin Luther King, Jr.'s concept of a just law; Who should feed and house the homeless?; Hobbes' state of nature and contemporary international law; Relationship of John Locke's views on human nature to his views on a fair society; Human rights and civil rights.

- *Metaphysics: The study of theories of reality.* Sample topics: Quantitative and qualitative accounts of nature in the pre-Socratic philosophers; Ancient and modern atomism; Must metaphysics be scientific?
- *Epistemology: The study of how humans can know, the kinds of knowledge, and the possibility of certainty.* Sample topics: Circularity in Descartes' *Meditations*; The subjectivity of scientific knowledge; Levels of certainty.
- *Philosophy of religion: The study of problems of knowledge and truth in religion.* Sample topics: Can empirical evidence prove the existence of God?; Concepts of the divine; Rational and irrational elements in prayer; R. M. Hare's concept of faith; Minds and souls.

Logic is the study of the rules of good reasoning. The content of logic courses varies. You may study symbolic logic, practical reasoning in everyday language, or something in between. Papers may be on topics in logic. They may also be thesis defense papers on topics of general interest.

Topics should not be so broad that they can't be examined thoroughly, or at least convincingly. "Plato" is too broad a topic. "Plato's ethics" is still too broad. Entire books can be dedicated to this vast topic. "The three-part soul in Plato's *Republic*" is a more workable topic, and you may have to get even more specific than this. You may narrow it down to "the relation between the four cardinal virtues and the three-part soul in Plato's *Republic*" or even focus on only one of those virtues, e.g., temperance.

Topics should not be so narrow that they are not worth writing about. In such cases, the topic is not interesting or contentious, or the topic yields insufficient discussion to warrant a paper. For example, a paper on how frequently a philosopher uses a certain word or expression is not worth the effort unless this inquiry somehow contributes to a more significant issue.

What You Will Find in This Book

In Chapter 2, you will encounter some basic concepts of writing papers and a detailed discussion of thesis defense papers, the most commonly assigned kind of paper in college philosophy classes. In Chapter 3 you will learn about the other kinds of papers mentioned earlier. You don't need to read about each kind, but you should read about thesis defense papers, even if you have been assigned a different kind of paper. Often, those other kinds turn out to be variant forms of the basic thesis defense paper.

In later chapters, you find hints on how to write and edit your paper. Research skills are also explained both for general resources and for those that are specific to the field of philosophy. Unless your professor instructs otherwise, your references—notes, works cited—should be in a standard format. The formats most frequently used in philosophy are illustrated in the sample citations in Chapter 6.

If you haven't done so already, look at the table of contents for this book. You will get a good idea of what sorts of help the book will afford you, and an overview of the text allows you to reference specific sections of the chapters quickly.

Good luck with your paper. Be sure you "make" most of that luck by doing your best work. Again, call to mind the opening advice:

Start right away.

2

Thesis Defense Papers

The **thesis defense paper,** sometimes called an argumentative paper, is the kind most often assigned in college philosophy classes. The paper topic may be one that deals with academic issues in philosophy. However, since philosophy courses on ethics may address not only the ideas of philosophers but also everyday issues and contemporary events, papers in those courses may not seem to be on "philosophy" in any technical sense. Also, since logic, which is one area of philosophy, aims at the improvement of basic and generic reasoning skills on any issue, papers for logic classes may focus on all sorts of topics in current affairs, human nature, and everyday life. So thesis defense papers for philosophy classes may be of three types, according to subject matter: pure philosophy, applied philosophy, and general topics.

In a thesis defense paper, you make a claim and give good reasons for believing that it is true. You defend your claim as you argue that much better reasons exist for accepting it than for rejecting it. You may not be able to prove your thesis is true, but you should try to show that an unbiased, clear-thinking person would have good reason to accept it.

Developing a Thesis

Thesis comes from an ancient Greek word that means *stand* or *position.* Your thesis is the stand or position you take on an issue.

In a thesis defense paper, you generally state your thesis at the beginning of the paper and then spend the remaining paragraphs and pages showing why that position is correct or reasonable.

A topic like *abortion* is not a thesis. A thesis is always given in sentence form. Although *abortion* is not a thesis, the following statement is: *Abortion is morally wrong in all cases, except when the mother's life can be saved by aborting a nonviable fetus.* So is this one: *Abortion of a fetus in the first trimester of pregnancy is the moral right of the woman.* Here are a few more sample theses:

> *The existence of God cannot be established through empirical evidence.*

> *The charge that Descartes' second and fifth* Meditations *display circular reasoning rests on a misunderstanding of his concept of God.*

> *The charge that Socrates criticized others' ideas but never offered ideas of his own is false. He offered a constructive philosophy of the morally justifiable life.* (Note: The thesis is stated in two sentences here, but it articulates a single idea.)

> *The Los Angeles riots were morally unjustifiable, but they were a result of unjust and chronic social inequities.* (Note: The author of a paper with this thesis has to establish two things: that the riots were unjustifiable and that they resulted from social inequities that were unjust and chronic.)

Some of these thesis statements can be used in what will be called, in this book, an analysis paper. As you will learn in Chapter 3, however, analysis papers often take a thesis defense form.

Choose a thesis that is worth the effort you will put into arguing for it. A position that hardly anyone would seriously disagree with, or an arguable position on a trivial issue, is not worth your time. You don't want to make your point, only to be met with a shrug of boredom: "So what?"

On the other hand, a very broad thesis may turn out to be too difficult to support. A paper on a grand topic achieves little for its author if the thesis has not been shown to be plausible. To show this, you need at least one good line of reasoning that rests on evidence from reliable sources. You may need to begin with a tentative thesis and search to find if supporting evidence is available. You may find after research that the opposing thesis is more defensible than the one tentatively selected!

Don't close your mind, staying with your original idea for a thesis if you see that you would have to suppress some evidence and overplay other evidence in order to defend it. Consider arguing for the opposing thesis instead, or qualifying the thesis to make it more defensible.

The Opening and Closing Paragraphs

You should make two things clear to the reader in the very first paragraph: precisely what your thesis is and how you intend to support it. Here is an example of an opening paragraph from a thesis defense paper.

Animal experimentation is necessary in the search for cures for human diseases, even though it sometimes causes pain and even death to the animals. Four basic points, to be argued for in this paper, lead to this conclusion. First, humans generally have a greater obligation to preserve human life than to preserve animal life. Second, some cures cannot be discovered in any other way. Third, despite popular misconception, very few of these experimental projects do in fact cause serious harm to the animals. Fourth, some of the experiments give us information about the animal species that ultimately is used to protect individuals of that species or the species itself.

The thesis statement is not always the first sentence of the opening paragraph. The preceding paragraph, for example, could have been introduced with one or more sentences describing the public controversy on this issue.

An opening paragraph in which you state the thesis and preview the reasoning is almost always required. For some professors, the thesis statement without the preview of arguments is sufficient. Unless informed otherwise, assume that your opening paragraph must state both the thesis and the main arguments.

In the closing paragraph, the author usually restates the thesis and reviews the main arguments. Thus it mirrors the opening paragraph. Here is a sample closing paragraph from a thesis defense paper.

It has been argued in this paper that we have a greater obligation to preserve human life than animal life, that some cures cannot be developed by other means, that animal experimentation usually does not seriously harm the animals, and that the animal species itself can benefit from some of this research. These points lead to the conclusion that animal experimentation is necessary in the search for cures for human diseases, despite the animal pain and death sometimes involved.

When writing your closing paragraph, always go back to the opening paragraph to ensure that you are now claiming to have done just what you promised, and refer to the rest of the paper itself to ensure that this is what you did establish. Sometimes an author establishes a worthy position in the paper but begins and/or ends with a thesis statement that is both grander and more difficult to support. What a shame. Now the author has not established the claim made in the thesis statement. This weakens the paper. Pay attention to the wording of the opening and closing paragraphs. Have you done what you said you would do?

The Body of the Paper

The body of the paper is everything between the opening and closing paragraphs. The structure of the body of a thesis defense paper should reflect the preview in the opening paragraph. If the sample opening paragraph from the preceding section of this chapter were your opening paragraph, then in the next group of paragraphs (perhaps set off by the roman numeral I) you should present reasons for believing that humans have a greater obligation to preserve human life than animal life. After you make your best case for that, in the following group of paragraphs (continue the roman numerals if you started them in the preceding section), you should give reasons for believing that some cures for human diseases cannot be discovered in other ways. The third (III) group of paragraphs should display the best reasoning you can offer for thinking that most animal experimentation causes little harm to the animals. The final (IV) group of paragraphs should support your final point: in this case, that animals themselves are sometimes aided by this research. (A point like this last one, which is not essential to your line of reasoning, should be included only if you can support it convincingly. You weaken your paper whenever you offer poorly supported opinion.)

The reader should know what you are trying to do in this part of the paper and how that relates to your conclusion, the thesis statement. Don't let the reader think, "I wonder what point this author is driving at?" If the structure of the body of your paper reflects your opening paragraph preview (covering the same matters in the same order), and if your closing paragraph is in keeping with both of these, the reader will be able to follow your reasoning more easily than if you make the reader read through part of the paper before figuring out what you're up to.

Make it even easier than that. When you shift from one point to another, use transition phrases to call attention to the shift. You can write, for example, "The second main argument in support of the thesis of this paper is that . . . ." Or you can write, "The next step in the line of reasoning that supports the thesis of this paper . . . ." As mentioned earlier, you can also divide your paper into sections with roman numerals or even titles to help the reader keep track of your points and recall how they relate to your thesis. If an intelligent, attentive reader is confused when reading the paper, you should have found a way to make it clearer. Providing good, clear reasoning is the author's job in a thesis defense paper. Do your job well.

Arguing for the Thesis

The author of a thesis defense paper argues for the claim that was made in the thesis statement. That thesis statement, re-member, expresses the assertion that the author intends to es-tablish as true or probably true. But notice the use of the word *argue:* the author "argues" for the claim.

In everyday discourse, people commonly use the word *argue* to describe heated, contentious advocacy of an idea. This popu-lar use of the expression may mislead in a discussion of thesis defense papers and reasoning in philosophy generally. In these cases, when someone says you must *argue, present an argument,* or *defend a thesis,* there is no intention to suggest that you are supposed to narrow your mind, become an angry adversary, or oversimplify. Instead, you are supposed to present well-reasoned thoughts about why the thesis is a credible one and to base your reasoning on good evidence. Your paper is weakened if it sounds as if you are wearing blinders. Philosophers, as much as thinkers in any other academic discipline, pride themselves on fairness in appraising even unpopular points of view, and the thesis defense paper is where we expect that this will be done in a careful and thorough way. Now consider some pointers on how to make a respectable argument for your thesis.

Tone

Don't allow yourself to sound like the worst stereotypes of politicians and advertisers. Don't try to sell your ideas with overblown rhetoric. Are you convinced by the politician or advertiser who obviously exaggerates the strengths of the favored view and the weaknesses of the disfavored one? No. Instead, you get the impression that persuasion is more important than accuracy and fairness to this opinionated or unprincipled advocate. You wouldn't be surprised to learn that supposedly factual claims were just fabricated.

This way of selling an idea or product won't work in academic writing either. The reader of your paper looks for good reasoning and reliable insights. It's a mistake to think that the author strengthens a thesis defense paper by wielding heavy-handed language or empty rhetoric. Sounding sure of yourself isn't the same as sounding reasonable, and the professor is unlikely to confuse the two.

An open-minded writer does not fabricate facts or play up evidence as if it establishes more than it actually does, so avoid the unrestrained language that suggests you might do this. An open-minded writer does not treat other views unfairly, so avoid undisciplined expressions that suggest that you are not above such contrivance. In a paper advocating a pro-choice position on abortion, don't refer to "anyone so foolish and insensitive to think that a woman has no right whatsoever over her own body." In a paper advocating a pro-life position on abortion, don't refer to "the degenerates who feel that their personal convenience is more important than a human life."

You earn credibility by the tone of your wording. If you sound as if you listen to reason rather than jump to conclusions, the reader has no reason to believe you are closed-minded. Your ideas will receive a better hearing. If you avoid extreme language that smacks of indignation, self-righteousness, and derision, the reader has no reason to discount what you have said before you finish your argument.

Kinds of Evidence

A reasonable tone sets the stage for good reasoning but, of course, it does not itself give anyone justification for believing you. It may give someone a reason for listening to you, but not a reason for believing you.

It is difficult to generalize about the difference between strong and weak evidence. To start with, let's just consider some examples. If you want to convince someone that a world government should replace the many different governments of present nations, some kinds of evidence will be more respectable than other kinds. The elimination of national rivalries that lead to wars and persecutions because of pettiness, vanity, and greed is an attractive advantage. Although others can respond with counterclaims—e.g., that these problems would be regionalized rather than eliminated, or that disadvantages would outweigh these advantages—this point can still be part of a good argument if it is presented well. On the other hand, you don't want to say that a world government should be created because it is inconvenient to have different traffic rules in various nations. The difficulties inherent in disestablishing the current nations and creating and maintaining a new world government are certainly not worth the effort for mere convenience in a relatively insignificant matter. Even the weightier moral argument that laws on capital punishment should not vary, condemning some and sparing others arbitrarily, may seem insufficient to justify attempting such a formidable task as reworking the politics of the world.

You can find entire books on how to reason well and avoid faulty inferences. For a strong focus on bias and fair reasoning, consider *Open Minds and Everyday Reasoning* (Wadsworth, 1993) by Zachary Seech, which also has a chapter on writing thesis defense papers. For a strong focus on reasoning in the social and political arena, try *Logic and Contemporary Rhetoric* (Wadsworth,

1992) by Howard Kahane. Another book worth your attention is *An Introduction to Reasoning* (Macmillan, 1984) by Steven Toulmin, Richard Rieke, and Allan Janik. All three of these books explore kinds of evidence and basic rules of reasoning.

Let us briefly survey several fundamental kinds of evidence that you can use to establish a claim as true and discuss how each is sometimes misused. Four kinds of evidence are considered: anecdotal, testimonial, statistical, and analogical.

Anecdotal evidence

When grand claims and unqualified generalizations are carelessly tossed about in conversation, we sometimes welcome **examples.** Talk is cheap. Examples bring the discussion down to earth and are refreshingly "factual" because they are based on observation rather than easy generalization. An **anecdote** is one sort of example. It is a short account of an interesting incident or event, especially one in the life of a person. One participant in a conversation might remark on how much better women are than men at some particular task. Another participant might then offer anecdotal counterevidence by observing that his father was much better at such tasks than his mother. Of course, someone else might have opposing anecdotal evidence.

How does anecdotal evidence really work? The basic rules are the same for reasoning in conversation and in writing. Obviously an anecdote, or another kind of example, cannot prove an *all* statement. Dad was better than mom at this task; that doesn't show that all men are better than women at it. So avoid treating a single case as proving a general point. Otherwise your reasoning will be weak. On the other hand, a single anecdote or counterexample is alone sufficient to *disprove* an *all* statement. If you say that women are always better at this task, my one anecdote shows that you have to modify your claim (unless you challenge the truth of my anecdote). So feel free to use reliable anecdotal evidence to critique universal claims.

The *all* statements referred to here may not employ the word "all." One can say instead that "*every* student wants to learn" or that "revolutions *always* occur only after an improvement in the general welfare." These are still universal statements that concede no exception.

Similarly, *most* statements may not actually employ the word "most." If we say that women or men or generally, usually, or normally "like that"—having some particular characteristic—what is the role of anecdote in the arguments we might employ? Clearly, the *most* statement allows for some contrary cases. An anecdote, however vividly presented, will not count as weighty evidence in support of such a statement or in opposition to it. Don't make the mistake of letting an example serve as an argument with statements like this.

Anecdotes and other examples can lend color and generate understanding. They are useful and not necessarily irrelevant. However, when you are writing a thesis defense paper, be sure you see the limitations of an anecdote as evidence.

Testimonial evidence

Whether they present themselves in conversation, writing, or silent reflection, your conclusions about people and the world will be quite restricted if you always refuse to rely on the reports of other people. Almost all of our knowledge of other countries, national events, or various professions and special occupations comes from what we have heard from others or what we have read. It would be silly for us to insist on believing only what we have personally experienced. In fact, it is difficult even to imagine how weird a person's life would be if he behaved as if only first-hand knowledge were reliable.

Of course, the opposite approach to the testimony of others is also perverse. Even in comedy we rarely get a chance to picture the radically gullible person who believes everything that anyone says without regard to the source. All of us lie between the extremes of complete self-reliance and indiscriminate credulity when it comes to matters of knowledge. Still, there are some fine lines to be drawn.

In a thesis defense paper, since you are showcasing your reasoning skills and boldly claiming the truth of your thesis, you must be careful not to accept blindly even the word of authorities, although the paper itself may involve some reference to them and even some reliance on them. People who get nationwide attention are not necessarily genuine authorities. Geraldo Rivera talks about sex topics regularly on his television show, and he interviews people with many sorts of unusual experiences. Yet his testimony on sexual psychology or morality would be worthless in an academic paper. He is not an expert in the field and should not be cited as one. The now famous "Dr. Ruth" is not as weak a source as Rivera because she has some training in the area and focuses much more on factual physiological research. Nevertheless, for a good academic paper you need to use top-flight sources. On sexual matters, Janet Hyde is an example of an authoritative source. She is Professor of Psychology at the University of Wisconsin and Director of the Women's Studies Research Center there. She is also a member of the Board of Directors of the National Council for Research on Women, editor of the *Psychology of Women Quarterly*, and a fellow of both the American Psychological Association and the Society for the Scientific Study of Sex. She has written a well-known textbook on human sexuality and has worked on several studies in developmental psychology.

The testimony of credible persons sometimes strengthens your argument, but you almost always need to say *why* the reader should especially consider that person's comments. Give credentials. These may include academic degrees and professional experience. Don't assume, however, that respectable credentials alone establish the fact that we should accept the testimony without question. You should know when experts disagree on an issue, so that one expert's assessment does not alone establish the point. You should also realize that credentials that impress people outside the field of expertise may be deceptive. The president of the American Society of Professional Psychologists will command less credibility if we know that he founded this tiny group and is its only officer. At the very least, we need more information about his credentials before judging the authority of this source. And on some issues, even expert opinion will not add much to your own reasoning. The thesis defense paper should involve your own thinking and be more than a compilation of quotes.

Use similar caution in citing publications. An unattributed article on sexual behavior in *Readers' Digest* or another popular magazine may be better ignored than mentioned, even if it supports your thesis. Although we all know that the printed and published word is not always truthful, many authors are tempted to use weak sources when good ones are not available. Does inclusion of the reference strengthen or weaken your paper? You have to use judgment. It varies with the topic, the source, and your line of argument. Popular magazines with light reading fare like *Cosmopolitan* and *People* seldom, if ever, provide anything to strengthen an argument in a philosophy paper, and the sensationalizing tabloid newspapers are never respectable sources of evidence. Some other popular magazines, such as *The Atlantic Monthly, Harper's,* and *The New Yorker* routinely publish articles with more analytical sophistication and depth. Still, you must consider each article on the basis of the author's credentials and the character of the written material itself.

Finally, avoid extensive quotes, and always give your own comment on the quote or reported view. Don't just report what the authority claims; say why the reader should seriously consider it.

Statistical evidence

When you fashion part of your argument with statistics, always report the source. Since statistics from different sources may vary or conflict, give reports from multiple sources when possible. And due to this possible variation or conflict, a stark mention of the results of "a recent study" does not address the issue of whether the results of the study are characteristic of other studies as well. Whenever possible, as you report your source, show that it is a reputable one. The reader will want to know that the researcher is competent and unbiased.

Report the year in which the statistics were compiled. Currency is usually important. And when you compare statistics from different years, be sure the criteria for compilation do not vary. If the rules have changed on how the U.S. government computes the Gross National Product or the rate of inflation, for example, you can't instructively compare figures compiled after the change to pre-change figures without statistical adjustment. (A similar criterion check is necessary when comparing different sources for similar information).

Analogical evidence

We use **analogies** to make points or illustrate ideas when we speak and when we write. In an analogy, we attempt to clarify one thing by comparing it with another that is similar in some way. Often the things compared are very different; they may be similar in only one respect.

In a simile, the wording includes an explicit expression of comparison. "His unusual cough was *like* the rattle of a loose ball bearing." In a metaphor, no explicit expression of comparison is used. "Housing developments of that sort are anthills." Similes and metaphors are simple kinds of analogies, but in argumentation we often reserve the term *analogy* for more complicated comparisons from which an insight or conclusion is to be drawn.

Analogies have been employed for ages. Plato, in Book *V* of his famous *Republic*, creates dialogue in which Socrates answers the question of whether women as well as men should hold the highest offices in an ideal political community. His response is the question: Would a bald man or a long-haired man be a better shoemaker? Obviously, hair distribution is a characteristic irrelevant to the cobbler's skill. Socrates suggests by analogy that gender is a characteristic irrelevant to skills of political leadership. Plato's *Republic* is full of argumentative analogies.

Analogies provide interest and rhetorical color to a line of reasoning. However, you must be cautious when you create your own analogy or evaluate someone else's. The logical power of an analogy is often overestimated. Usually an analogy will help a person understand a relation and see new connections between things, but seldom does it provide hard proof of a conclusion or thesis for a person who ardently resists that view. Analogies are especially useful for articulating a new perspective that has just been supported with empirical evidence, because they often illustrate rather than establish points of view.

Premises, Conclusions, and Transitions

A reader may confuse the author's premises and conclusions if these are not carefully distinguished. A premise is any statement of evidence. A conclusion is any statement for which evidence has been offered.

Clearly, your thesis statement is a conclusion. The purpose of a thesis defense paper is the presentation of evidence for that statement. You will probably have other conclusions in your paper as well. The several main points that together are meant to demonstrate the truth of your conclusion will almost certainly be supported by further specific evidence. Thus the statements that directly support the conclusion are both premises (since they constitute the reasons for believing the thesis) and conclusions (since evidence is presented for *those* statements). You can think of your thesis as the *ultimate conclusion.* It is supported then by *transitional conclusions* that are both premise and conclusion, enabling you to make a transition from your secondary argumentation to your primary one. The primary argumentation is the move from the transitional conclusions to the ultimate conclusion or thesis statement.

For an example, consider the line of reasoning illustrated in the preceding sections, "The Opening and Closing Paragraphs" and "The Body of the Paper." The thesis and ultimate conclusion, fully stated, was "Animal experimentation is necessary in the search for cures for human diseases, even though it sometimes causes pain and even death to the animals." The four transitional conclusions previewed in the opening paragraph were the "four basic points to be argued for in this paper." These are supported one at a time in the body of the paper with the best evidence the author can supply. A good paper has both a clear structure and compelling evidence.

When you shift between stating evidence and conclusion (whether transitional or ultimate), you should make the shift very clear. Moves that are obvious to you because you already know what you intended to say may be unclear to a reader. So make good use of *conclusion indicators* and *premise indicators.*

Conclusion indicators are expressions that often precede and serve to announce a conclusion. *So, thus, therefore,* and *consequently* are words that perform this function. In addition, there is the less common *hence* and innumerable phrases such as *this leads us to the conclusion that* and *it follows that.*

Premise indicators are expressions that often precede and serve to announce a premise. *Since* and *because* are the most common premise indicators in both spoken and written English. Various phrases like *due to the fact that* and *for the following reasons* also introduce premises.

You can also use entire sentences to signal major shifts from one argument to another. You might write, for example, "We have now considered the evidence for the first of the three main points to be offered in support of the thesis that private individuals should not be allowed to possess handguns or semiautomatic weapons. Let us move on to the second point." In this case, a pair of sentences proclaims a shift that no attentive reader can miss.

The reader should not only be able to understand the sentence being read but also know how you intend to relate it to the sentences and paragraphs around it and in the rest of the paper.

Presenting Another Side

A thesis defense paper may include counterarguments. These counterarguments may be arguments that a critic might level directly at your thesis without attention to the specific arguments that you have offered in support of your thesis. These counterarguments may instead be arguments that a critic might use to discredit one of the specific lines of reasoning with which you have supported your thesis.

Why would you include arguments against the point of view you have adopted? After all, the purpose of the thesis defense paper is to present the strongest case *for* your thesis, and the rule on what to include in the paper dictates that only what supports the thesis statement merits inclusion.

The answer is that you do strengthen your case by giving voice to counterarguments *if* you can respond to these concerns with good reasoning. By demonstrating that you have anticipated the concerns of people who would critique your views, you can avoid giving the reader the sense that you are smugly self-assured and thoroughly unappreciative of other perspectives on the issue. When you fail to bring up a likely objection to your position or your reasoning, you allow the reader to conclude that you simply do not have a good answer to it—or that you are unaware of it. A good answer can neutralize that objection in the reader's mind and allow your own arguments to be more persuasive.

It does you no good to make up weak counterarguments that insightful critics would never employ. The objections that you anticipate in your paper should be credible ones. They can be critical comments that you have come up with on your own, noting what others may perceive as weak points. You might introduce such a critique by writing, "A critic may object to this line of reasoning on the following grounds." Then you explain the concern and respond to it. On the other hand, the objections may be ones that have actually been offered by others in the face of views similar to yours. You can introduce them in this sort of way: "Professor Moreno has objected to this kind of argument in her book *Social Fallacies* by saying. . . ." You can also make up an objection along the lines that would probably be pursued by a particular thinker. For example, you might write, "A. J. Ayer would almost certainly object to this argument because it is based on. . . ." In such a case, you would project from the writings of that author to a specific argument of your own. Be sure you do not misrepresent the views of that author. When you respond, do not sound intolerant and do not oversimplify the concern. If it is a sufficiently important counterargument to be included in your paper, then it will deserve respectful attention. If the objection has some merit, you can acknowledge that without "giving away the farm"—that is, without conceding all aspects of the critique.

If you intend to include one or more counterarguments to your position or reasoning, consider announcing your intention in the opening paragraph. Of course, if the contended point is a relatively minor aspect of your reasoning, the counterargument may not warrant opening-paragraph status.

Fallacies and Sidetracks

We all reason well most of the time. In most of the routine matters of living, we draw conclusions quite reliably. But when our biases are in full flower and we try too hard to maintain one perspective and resist another, we can fail to recognize errors in our reasoning that would otherwise stand out clearly. Watch out for the following fallacies and sidetracks.

A **false dilemma** is created when the author presents two alternatives as if they are the only ones possible, when in fact a third alternative exists. The reasoning offered by the creator of the false dilemma is this: If one of these alternatives is not true, then the other has to be true. But the simple either/or statement masks other possibilities. For example, an author carried away by blinding fervor for the thesis that capital punishment should be employed actively in all states of the union might proclaim that "we must universally adopt capital punishment unless we want crime running rampant and unchecked in every street." Is it true that without capital punishment, law and order will not be enforced anywhere in the nation? An inclination toward overstatement has set up what seems to be a false dilemma. Certainly, the author must modify the wording or argue specifically that the dilemma is not false and that this is the only possible alternative to the practice of capital punishment.

Extremism had a role in the preceding false dilemma. Avoid adopting such extreme points of view that you can defend them only by closing your mind, overstating the case for your position, and unfairly attacking opposing positions and arguments.

You set up a **straw man** whenever you attack a misrepresentation of someone's position or argument. For example, a straw man or counterfeit stand is attacked when a person who advocates the regulation of handguns is criticized as if she had proposed banning all handguns—a more radical (and different!) proposal. Straw men that are easier to attack than the actual position or argument are sometimes set up on purpose to make a weak case appear stronger. Often, however, they simply result from inattention or inadequate inquiry into that person's ideas.

A **tangent** is a side topic that, although related to the topic under discussion, is carried in directions that are not relevant to that discussion topic. When you are writing a paper, be wary of those aspects of the topic that you want to include (for whatever reason) but which have no proper place in the paper. In some kinds of writing, it's hard to tell when you're going off on a tangent, writing about something related to the main topic but not closely enough related to be included. In a thesis defense paper, there is a simple rule for what to include: *If it's good evidence for your conclusion or for one of the main points that you are using to support your conclusion, then include it in your paper. If it's related to your topic and interesting but doesn't provide more reason for believing the conclusion, then leave it out.*

The **fallacy of common belief** is committed when the author supports a claim that is not self-evidently true by observing that many people believe it to be true. False beliefs about the nature of the world, the human psyche, and certain races of people were at one time widespread. That did not make them true. Sometimes the grand claim that "everybody knows" is the disarming preface to such a claim.

The **fallacy of two wrongs make a right** is committed when an action is justified only by identifying another, usually similar, action that someone else has taken. Clearly, as our parents told us years ago, one wrong doesn't justify a second one. You are not blameless for doing something shameful just because someone else did it first. Nevertheless, in politics and on various social topics, adults continue to commit this childhood fallacy. In your paper, don't argue that one act is defensible on the grounds that some others have acted similarly.

In the **fallacy of contrary-to-fact hypothesis,** someone makes unknowable claims about what would have resulted if some event in the past had been different. For example, unqualified statements about how John F. Kennedy's presidency would have been viewed by future Americans if he had not been assassinated are statements that should be challenged. The same is true of claims about the results of the war in the Persian Gulf had anti-Iraqi forces moved on to Baghdad or had they remained as a stronger presence in the area. Speculation about such things is certainly understandable, and reasons can be given for particular conclusions. However, when arguing in a thesis defense paper, do not state with an unreasonable degree of certainty the results of events that might have occurred but did not.

The **fallacy of questionable cause** is committed when, on insufficient evidence, we identify a cause for something that happened or a fact that is true. Next to the false dilemma, this is probably the most common fallacy. We name one thing as the cause of another when there may have been other causes; we simply overlook the other possibilities. Why did the L.A. riots of 1992 occur? What caused the decline in college entrance test scores over the past decades? Very often, the problem is not just that we latch onto the wrong cause. It's that we name as the sole cause something that is one of several contributing causes. In either of these versions, you have the ever-popular fallacy of questionable cause. In a rush to write a dynamic paper, don't fall prey to this kind of misassessment or oversimplification. If what you identify as a causal agent is a probable cause, and if you can make a good case for that, don't call it the certain cause. If what you identify is a contributing cause, don't brand it as the lone cause, even if the exact mix of contributing causes eludes you. Claim only as much as you can credibly defend.

3

Other Kinds of Papers

Thesis defense papers are the kind of assignment for which philosophy classes are known. They call for the sorts of reasoning skills and conceptual analyses that are at the heart of philosophy. Thesis defense papers are not the only kind of written work assigned in philosophy classes, however. Many professors assign work that is subtly or even strikingly different from the assignments of their neighboring professors.

In this chapter, because of the wide spectrum of assignments for papers, we examine several other basic kinds of papers that are assigned in philosophy classrooms. These are:

- Compare-and-contrast papers
- Analysis papers
- Research papers
- Summary papers and abstracts

Even if you have been assigned one of the kinds of papers that is dealt with specifically in this chapter and you have not been assigned a thesis defense paper, do read Chapter 2 on thesis defense papers. Some of the general pointers about paper writing are covered there. Furthermore, as you will soon discover, each of these kinds, except for the last (summary papers and abstracts), is often best presented in a thesis defense format. Even in the last kind, it is often necessary to identify that writer's thesis and argumentation.

Compare-and-Contrast Papers

In any written assignment, you should pay attention to the verbs used in the description of your task. The words *explain, analyze, identify, compare, contrast, illustrate, summarize, locate, arrange, justify, define, prove, describe,* and *recount* refer to different sorts of tasks. Each is used to ask you to do something different. The wording of an assignment sometimes includes more than one of these expressions. In these cases, you must be especially careful to read attentively, distinguish all the terms from one another, and perform each of the assigned tasks.

One common kind of paper is the **compare-and-contrast paper.** Students may be asked to compare and contrast (1) the ideas of specific philosophers named by the professor, (2) the ideas of any philosophers in a particular philosophical movement, with the selection made by the student, (3) philosophical movements or schools of thought, (4) specific books by different authors, (5) specific books by the same author, and (6) the ways that one concept is developed in different times, by different thinkers or groups of thinkers. Examine an example of each of these:

> Compare and contrast the political views of John Locke and Thomas Hobbes.
>
> Compare and contrast the ethical thought of one utilitarian and one intuitionist.
>
> Compare and contrast logical positivism and ordinary language philosophy.
>
> Compare and contrast *The Trial* by Franz Kafka and *The Castle* by Albert Camus.
>
> Compare and contrast Plato's *Charmides* and his *Laches.*
>
> Compare and contrast the concept of utopia as developed by St. Thomas More and by Edward Bellamy.

The sort of subject exemplified by the last of these is often easiest to address because it specifies both the topic and the thinkers, thus limiting the range of material you must synthesize and analyze. Notice that the first of the examples would have been much more specific if it were of this sort. The instructions might have read: Compare and contrast the concepts of a social or political state of nature as developed by John Locke and Thomas Hobbes.

The search for comparisons and contrasts is, of course, nothing more than an attempt to find what is similar and what is different about the two things being compared. Many of the dissimilarities will be obvious. If you are familiar with the things to be compared, you will almost certainly notice some things that can be said of one but not the other. If you do not discern differences, you probably need to do more reading to familiarize yourself with the details of the ideas involved in the assignment.

The similarities may be more difficult to recognize. If you do discover that the two things you have to compare seem to have little in common, try thinking about very general aspects. Perhaps the thinkers or philosophies that are being compared share at least some unstated assumptions about human motivation, political rights, mental capacities, language, emotion, personal fulfillment, or some other important notions relevant to the comparison. The things being compared almost always have something in common, some point of agreement or similarity.

What will provide a focus for the compare and contrast paper? In what way will the paper hang together and be grasped as a unity by the reader, rather than read just as a series of comments on various similarities and dissimilarities? One way of providing such unity is to preview your comparative paper with a short account of the general ways that the compared things are the same and the general ways that they are different. Generalize and give an overview of your assessment.

When you do this, you almost transform this kind of paper into a thesis defense paper like the ones described in Chapter 2. You might profitably take the extra step and create a thesis statement, completing the transformation. In the thesis statement you should proclaim your assessment, saying generally how the two things being compared are similar and how they are not. While some compare-and-contrast papers are not written in an explicit thesis defense format, your professor may require it and, even if it is not required, it may turn out to be a useful way to organize and present your paper. Consider several sample statements:

Plato's ideal society as presented in the *Republic* and Edward Bellamy's as presented in *Looking Backward* share several definitive assumptions about the character of good citizens and healthy relations between social groups, but they diverge significantly on desirable political structures of styles of living.

Plato and Bellamy agree that social conditions greatly influence the character of interactions in a society, but they disagree on the extent to which divergent individual traits can be changed.

Plato and Bellamy share the belief that personal wealth and acquisitiveness must be controlled in any society that is to avoid corruption, but they differ on which social policies could bring about such a change in people and on whether such a change could be universal.

The remainder of the paper's opening paragraph may preview the sorts of evidence to be offered. Then the philosophers' general positions and specific passages from their writings can be offered as evidence for—as "reasons for believing"—each of these claims.

If you do not word your compare-and-contrast paper as a thesis defense, there is another structural issue to consider. Should you, in the first half of the paper, deal with one of the two things to be compared, and then compare and contrast as you present the parallel aspects of the second? Or should you move back and forth between the two, comparing one aspect of each at a time?

Generally, the second of these approaches is better. Why? With the first approach, you don't engage the reader immediately in the activity of comparing and contrasting, which is both engaging and the purpose of the paper. The reading is more likely to be tedious. Also, with the first approach, you may make it necessary for some readers to continually return to the first part of the paper to remember what you wrote there about each aspect that is being considered in the second part. This is awkward and irksome. If you do lots of reminding in the second part in order to avoid this problem, you become redundant. That can be bothersome too.

One hybrid approach calls for a short summary of each of the two things to be compared, followed by a comparative section. It is also hard to do this well. Short summaries do not give a basis for an in-depth comparison, and long summaries are tedious and require that the heart of the paper be deferred to the end.

Despite the generalizations made here, each of these structures for a compare-and-contrast paper may be more workable than the others for a certain topic. Do not make a final decision on the paper's structure until you consider what it will take to deal with the specific material and highlight the desired points.

Analysis Papers

You may be required to write a paper in which you *analyze* a concept, a philosopher's views, or a philosophical book or article. The kind of paper we call an **analysis paper** is the kind that calls for a close examination of a concept or some writings and a carefully reasoned examination of various aspects of it. Analysis involves considering basic elements or aspects of something in order to better understand the whole thing.

Sometimes a philosophical concept is analyzed (with or without reference to what has already been written on the subject). Take as an example the philosophical concept of determinism, the notion that no events, including human actions, could have occurred differently from the way they did unless preceding or simultaneous conditions were different. In other words, there are no free actions, and human choice, as commonly understood ("I could haven chosen differently"), is an illusion. An analysis of determinism could examine various things, such as our everyday conception of free will, the current understanding of neurochemical brain processes, and case studies of decisions that have been made or might be made.

Sometimes a philosopher's writings on a certain subject are analyzed. It would be too great a task to analyze any philosopher's entire body of writings in a single paper unless this philosopher left very little for us to read. Often, it is even insufficient to limit the examination of a philosopher to one subject. For example, John Dewey wrote so much about education that a single short paper on his views on education would be too general. An author writing on this topic would do well to choose one aspect of his philosophy of education. The same is true of Jean Jacques Rousseau on politics, Kierkegaard on religion, or Kant on perception and thought.

Finally, books or articles that are philosophically significant are sometimes analyzed in papers for philosophy classes (and also in papers by professional philosophers who critique the work of their colleagues and peers). A short book like Robert Paul Wolff's *In Defense of Anarchy* can be reviewed and analyzed in an analysis paper, but here, as before, it is easier to limit the paper to one aspect of the book. Philosophical articles may be written so concisely, with lots of meaning packed into a paragraph, sentence, or even a clause, that they require attentive reading and rereading. But they are usually easy to digest in the sense that they usually have an explicit and well-defined thesis to guide the reader. The typical article by a professional philosopher is a thesis defense paper with a clearly stated thesis. A representative example is Elizabeth L. Beardsley's well-known article, "Determinism and Moral Perspectives" (published in the journal *Philosophy and Phenomenological Research*, XXI, 1960, pp. 1–20). Her thesis statement cannot be missed: "In this paper, I shall argue that judgments of moral praise and blame, affirmative as well as negative, can be made within the framework of determinism, provided that we accept a more complex account of these judgments and their foundations than is normally supplied or assumed."

So you are to analyze a concept, a philosopher's views, a book, or an article. The professor may give you a specific assignment: Analyze this topic or that article. Or the professor may invite you to think of something to analyze that relates to the course content. What kind of examination of its various aspects is expected? You should recognize and explain the more important strengths and weaknesses in the philosopher's writings or in one perspective on the philosophical concept that is being examined. You can address clarity, reasoning, evidence, assumptions, and implications. Show which are strengths or weaknesses by citing and discussing examples. You should also recognize and explain any interesting internal or external relations. Internal relations include consistency, coherence, and organization. External relations include connections—affinities or tensions—with the ideas of others.

Again, consider using a thesis defense format even if it is not required. This will help your reader, and that is always good. The author's intention should be to make things clear rather than to mystify or obscure.

Research Papers

A research paper is any paper for which you must locate and examine information from multiple sources. The specific sources to be used may be indicated in the professor's wording of the assignment. Usually they are not; you are expected to identify and find relevant resources on your own.

Research papers normally sandwich the body of the paper between an introduction and a closing paragraph, as most other kinds of papers do. However, there are additional parts to a research paper. You must have a final page or set of pages that is titled "Works Cited" or "Bibliography." A "Works Cited" section displays information such as author, publisher, and date of publication for each source to which you referred in your paper. The correct way to record this information is explained in Chapter 6. The "Works Cited" section is sometimes titled "Bibliography" (or "Works Consulted"), especially when you want to list works that were helpful to you but to which you did not actually refer in the paper. (Works may refer not only to books and articles but also to musical scores, speech texts, and non-print sources like video and audio productions.) Occasionally, a paper includes a list of cited works as well as a bibliography of other sources that were consulted and contributed to the author's general understanding of the topics addressed. Sometimes a section titled "Endnotes" (or just "Notes") is included. This is for the commentary notes and references to sources that would have been footnotes if they had been placed at the bottom of pages rather than in that "Endnotes" section. These references are numbered with a superscript—a number raised above the regular level of the type—in the text of the paper and at the beginning of each note. Generally, a paper will have either a format that employs endnotes or a list of works cited with parenthetical references to them through the text, but not both. See Chapter 6 for more on these formats. Research papers sometimes also have a section called an "Appendix." Here you place a graph, chart, document, or explanation that was too extensive, or perhaps too incidental, to include in the body of the paper, but which the reader may find useful. If more than a single appendix is attached, they should be designated "Appendix A," "Appendix B," and so on. The appendixes are placed before the Endnotes, Works Cited, or Bibliography pages. Finally, the bibliographic section may be annotated. That is, each work listed may be described briefly. The annotation is usually no more than several sentences or a paragraph long.

Of course, compare-and-contrast papers may involve some, or even much, research. Analysis papers, whether centered on a concept, philosopher, or text, may also involve research. The papers assigned in college philosophy classes are often combinations of the simple types described in this chapter. And certainly a research paper may also have a thesis defense structure.

The research for a philosophy paper is usually library research. Often, however, the library searches can be augmented by contacts you can make with people in the field about which you are writing. People who are reliable authorities can give you worthwhile testimony of their own or refer you to other sources. For example, the author of a paper on environmental policies might consult officials in the U. S. Department of the Interior or recognized naturalists. The author of a paper on relationships between mind and body might consult a chemistry professor, a scholarly physician, or a scientist working in that subfield. The author of a paper on the philosophy of sport might find helpful a conversation with coaches or athletes in professional sports or in Olympic competition.

Modern library technology has made library research easier. With computer cataloging, for example, digging for information in the library is a quicker and surer task than it has ever been. In Chapter 7 we discuss research skills and sources for inquiry into general and philosophic subjects.

Your research paper may involve both *primary sources* and *secondary sources*. Primary sources are books or articles that are a writer's original work—perhaps in translation, however, from another language—on a subject about which you are writing a paper. Secondary sources are books or articles *about* the philosopher or book or article that is a primary source. An example will help. Gilbert Ryle wrote a book titled *The Concept of Mind*. If your paper is on Ryle, reductionism, mental processes, or Ryle's book itself, then this can be a primary source for your paper. If you find an article by someone else, reviewing and evaluating Ryle, or even a section of a book in which Ryle's ideas in *The Concept of Mind* are summarized, you have a secondary source for that paper. For some assignments, students are asked to read only primary source material. Often they are expected to use both primary and secondary sources. Seldom is a paper to be forged only from secondary sources.

Summary Papers

In this book we call these papers **summary papers.** Many professors do not call them papers at all. They are simply summaries of primary source materials.

Students may be instructed to summarize or paraphrase the first of Descartes' six *Meditations.* They may be instructed to summarize John Stuart Mill's *Utilitarianism,* or William James' essay, *Pragmatism,* or one or more of the twelve parts of David Hume's *Dialogues Concerning Natural Religion.* With this sort of assignment, the professor intends to evaluate the students' understanding of the philosopher's position and arguments, rather than to evaluate their ability to offer their own critique of those ideas.

Do not begin to write a summary of a philosophic text—or any other text, for that matter—before you have finished reading it. Why? A summary is not intended to be a sentence-by-sentence rewriting of the original. It is not intended even to have the same number of paragraphs as the original. Often, the opening paragraphs do not get to the heart of the matter. They may be introductory and even incidental to the main argument. You need to know where the author is going, what the thesis and main lines of reasoning are. Idiosyncrasies of that author's style of writing or presentation should not show in your summary. Therefore, you need to know the entire passage to be summarized before you begin writing. A peculiar or self-indulgent style may be the right of the author of the original passage, but a summary should be clear and focused and should not draw attention to *its* author. So don't just change the turns of phrase or use synonyms to alter the word choice. You can pack that author's ideas into much less space because you are presenting only the essentials of that document. You can actually rewrite individual sentences without understanding what the author is up to, and that understanding is precisely what your professor wants to confirm. For specifics on how to phrase your writing, avoiding stiff wording and common errors, read on through Chapter 5.

Don't expect to be able to articulate perfectly the views of a philosopher after a single reading. Even several readings may be insufficient if you are reading straight through the book, chapter, or article as if it were part of a novel. In academics, where subtle differences in wording can be crucial (and the writing style is sometimes frustrating!), we—both students and professors—usually have to study paragraphs, not just read them. We constantly ask questions like, "How does this sentence relate to the preceding or following one?" and "What did that long sentence (that I just read) with so many clauses mean?" We keep stopping to reread sentences and ask if we still are clear about what the author is trying to prove and how one point is meant to support another. Outline what you read, take notes, and see whether you can compose an abstract. An abstract is an extremely brief summary of one to several paragraphs, stating the thesis and main lines of argument. It is somewhat like a good opening paragraph and only slightly more detailed.

You may find that even when you are not asked to write a summary paper on some writing you must master, it may be worth the effort for your own purposes. Composing an abstract or summary paper clarifies the author's argumentation in your own mind, and it provides a tool for reviewing that written piece and recalling it after time has passed and you have been distracted by chemistry classes, psychology classes, and everyday life.

You may encounter other writing projects in philosophy classes also. Journals and notebooks are sometimes assigned. Both the content and the format of these vary so widely that guidelines on writing them cannot be ventured here. The professor who assigns the work will provide instructions. Finally, you may be asked to write a reaction paper. In a reaction paper, you generally express subjective reactions to the material that you have read. Justification is usually not required. You may choose to report on any personal reaction, emotional or intellectual.

4

Writing the Paper

Start right away.

This was the advice you received on the first page of Chapter 1. You were told that you should make sure you understand the assignment and the criteria for evaluation. You were told to make a work schedule for the paper and plan interlibrary loans, interviews, computer access, and reading time so you don't run out of time at the end. This is all good advice. But don't slip into self-deception as you spend time on these preparatory activities. Don't keep busy with the planning, researching, and organizing while you put off the actual writing until the last minute. It is very common to delay the writing with the belief (or rationalization) that, even halfway to the due date for the paper, you are just "not ready to write yet." Although you do need to gather information, develop a tentative thesis, and plan the body of your paper, you should also consider the *start right away* advice to apply to the writing too.

Even if you have to start with very subjective pre-research paragraphs related to the topic you are investigating, start within a week of receiving the assignment (earlier if you have less than a couple weeks to the due date) and write something. Perhaps you won't use your early musings in your final draft, or even in your first full rough draft, but it will help you refine your thinking on the topics you are considering, and it is likely that you will end up with ideas to keep and develop as well as sentences and paragraphs to discard. This pre-writing may take as little as 15 minutes a day.

In this chapter, we review the first steps in forming a paper: choosing a topic, gathering information, and shaping a thesis. We also cover another preparatory step, outlining. Then we get to the writing itself. We discuss the rough and final drafts that any well-developed paper goes through. We also discuss writing style. There is some discussion about word processing on personal computers to develop, format, and print a paper.

Getting Started

Let's review the initial steps for creating a paper. If a specific paper topic has not been assigned, you must decide on a subject. Sometimes you will get an idea that sounds great but is unworkable because the supporting evidence and arguments that were expected to be available are not. You go to the library but you don't find the needed kind or amount of information. Or your anticipated lines of reasoning are not convincing when they are put down on paper. This happens to the best of professional writers, so don't let it lead you to the conclusion that you are on track for failure. These false starts are part of the business of writing. (Last minute composition, when you do not have time for false starts, compounds the frustration.)

If you are allowed to choose your topic, try to settle on one that genuinely interests you. When you choose a topic that was mentioned as an example in class, but in which you have no personal interest, writing a paper soon becomes tedious. Besides, people tend to write better papers when their enthusiasm amplifies their energies and sharpens their thinking. Having to be thorough and precise is demanding even when the topic is one for which you have an affinity. You set yourself up for mediocrity if you select a topic that bores you even before you start writing.

Should you try to select a topic and then gather information on it to find whether it is workable, or should you do some exploratory reading in the library in order to settle on a topic? The answer is that it varies with topics, assignments, and writers. Sometimes you know right away just what you would like to write on, sometimes you have a general idea, and sometimes you don't have a clue. However, assuming that you are employing a thesis defense structure, take care not to become inflexible about your thesis. Look up the relevant sources of information to see if you can make a good case for the thesis that you are considering. If your thesis is not defensible as you have worded it, change the wording. If this is not enough, change your stand on the issue, or change the thesis altogether while you stay with the same topic. If this thesis is also unworkable, or if you have other reasons for not wanting to defend this new thesis, change topics and begin the search for a thesis again. Even if your paper is not a thesis defense, this flexibility during the investigation of the topic helps you decide on your specific focus on the topic.

As you progress far into the writing of the paper, you may find that even subtle adjustments to the wording of the thesis—or adjustments to the focus of the paper—may be required. If you read an essay question on a test and fail to recheck the wording of the question, you may either answer a slightly different question or give only a partial answer to the question. Similarly, when you are feeling rushed and write the body of the paper without sufficient attention to the relation of the thesis to its support, the result will be a bungled project. The paper will be weak and perhaps unpassable.

Don't get lazy. Revise that thesis as often as you have to!

Outlining

A planning outline of a paper provides a plan that enables you to envision the entire project as intended before you write the first full-length draft. This outline displays what you expect to be the skeleton of paper, with the main points and subpoints laid out clearly in relation to each other and to the rest of the paper. The planning outline is fashioned as you do your early research. It can guide your continuing research and argumentation, reminding you where you need more supporting evidence and helping you assess the strength of the overall argument.

Even before putting together the planning outline, you can prethink the argumentation to be used in the paper, especially if it has a thesis defense structure. (Remember that compare-and-contrast papers, analysis papers, and research papers often have a thesis defense structure.) As you ponder the strongest ways to argue for your tentative thesis, map out these lines of reasoning by drawing a downward arrow from evidence to conclusion. You begin your map of the projected reasoning by writing the thesis near the bottom of a clean sheet of paper. For each separate reason for believing the conclusion, write that reason somewhere above the conclusion and draw a downward arrow to the thesis. If one reason for believing the conclusion (the thesis statement) has to be stated with several sentences, draw a plus sign (+) between those sentences, bracket them all, and then draw the downward arrow. For example, the thesis, still in rough form, that you are considering may be "Euthanasia for unconscious or mentally impaired patients should be decided by the patient's family." You begin by writing this in the lower section of a sheet of paper. You then ask yourself why this might be a good proposal. This thought occurs to you: The family knows the patient's character and wishes better than anyone. You reflect for a moment, then add the word *usually*: the patient's family usually knows the patient's character and wishes better than anyone. You write this above the thesis statement, but to the left so you have space to add other reasons. You draw a downward arrow from that sentence to the thesis statement. You reflect again. It is also the family that bears most of the consequences of the decision. After all, they are the ones to deal with the emotional effects of the daily absence of that person from their lives. And the people who are affected most, you reason, should make the decision. These reasons are written in toward the right of the previous one, and another downward arrow is drawn. The map of this initial reasoning is shown in Figure 1.

The plus sign between the two sentences on the right along with the bracket that groups them shows that these two work together to establish *a single reason* for believing the conclusion is true. They combine to make one point; each shows why the other sentence is relevant. So they have one arrow for the one inference. The arrow on the left represents a different inference: the one about knowing how the patient would feel about the situation and what the patient would want.

You can carry this mapping further. If you want to record some reasons for believing that any of the top three sentences are true, you can write those reasons above and draw an arrow

Figure 1

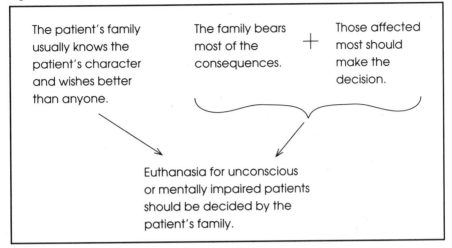

The patient's family usually knows the patient's character and wishes better than anyone.

The family bears most of the consequences.

Those affected most should make the decision.

Euthanasia for unconscious or mentally impaired patients should be decided by the patient's family.

down to that sentence. An extensive map can provide you with everything that you would place in an outline. You can go straight from the map to the outline and have the structure of your paper established.

Two more points should be made about mapping your reasoning. First, it is fine to do early maps by abbreviating sentences rather than writing them out. "Family bears consequences" is sufficient to remind you of your point. Second, maps are useful during the working stage as well. When you are researching and revising your reasoning, maps can help you visualize the current state of your argument so you can continue to work without losing track of the big picture.

An outline itself may be written with either full sentences or phrases. Using an outline, you can structure your paper before you write it. A thorough outline often designates each paragraph in the paper. The main sections of the paper—opening paragraph, closing paragraph, and each main point in the body of the paper—are labeled with roman numerals. Each of these sections is divided into at least two sections labeled with capital arabic letters. Each of these, in turn, is divided into at least two sections, labeled with numbers. Further subdivisions are marked with lower case arabic letters. The following chart may help.

I.   Opening paragraph
   A. Thesis statement
   B. Main points to be argued for in support of the thesis
      1. Point one
      2. Point two
      3. Point three
II. First main point
   A.
      1.
      2.
   B.
   C.
III. Second main point
   A.
   B.
IV. Third main point
   A.
      1.
         a.
         b.
      2.
   B.
V.   Closing paragraph
   A. Restatement of thesis
   B. Restatement of main points supporting the thesis
      1.
      2.
      3.

As you can see from the chart, you may have more than two divisions in a category (e.g., A, B, C; 1, 2, 3; a, b, c, d), and it is acceptable to have one item in a level (e.g., A) subdivided although another item of the same level (e.g., B) is not.

The planning outline becomes a working outline as you allow yourself to alter parts of it throughout the process of researching and writing the paper. Sometimes you find that you cannot argue effectively for one of the claims in your outline. You then have to change the claim, replace that argument, or delete it. Sometimes you decide that the paper needs to be reorganized because what you originally placed as a subheading under heading III fits better under IV. Occasionally you may conclude that what had seemed important to include in the paper really adds little or no strength to the overall argument. It may be an interesting tangent that doesn't belong in the paper at all.

There may be no need for a final outline. A final outline is a working outline that has been revised to show all the changes that were made, even if they were made as you transcribed the final draft. Final outlines are usually composed only when the class assignment requires an outline to be submitted with the paper. When this is required, the outline should be double spaced and placed immediately after the cover sheet unless the professor instructs otherwise.

Rough and Final Drafts

Don't let your first draft be your last draft. Nobody writes that well. Some people are surprised when they discover that even great authors revise, rewrite, and edit their work, and that this can be really difficult and sometimes frustrating work for them. Writing comes from the mind and often the heart. These are not the same in any two people. So what you write will be different from what another person would write on the same subject. Still, to do the best writing you can do, you have to prethink, write, rethink, and rewrite. With careful attention to your own work, you will find discrepancies between what you wrote and what you meant. Or you will find that your first thoughts are not your best thoughts. Maybe you write well enough to get an acceptable grade on fewer rewrites than it would take to do your best work, but it's only your best work—or something close to it—that you can feel really proud of when you put your name on the cover sheet.

Authors of college papers (and others) may delay the writing stage—which, you remember, should start early—because they fear their writing will not be good. So they acquire a sort of writer's block. They are unable to start writing. One cure to try if you are afflicted with such a malady is this: *Give yourself permission to write poorly!* That means you should let yourself put words down on paper without thinking about whether the result will be something you are willing to share with another person—if that is what it takes to get you started. Decide that, after writing one page, you will read it over and then choose whether to roll the paper up in a ball and toss it in the trash basket. If you do toss it, no one will have seen your words except you. You can start over on that day or another as if it were the first time. However, the chances are good that some ideas, sentences, or turns of phrase will be worth keeping. If nothing else, you will learn about some dead ends, and this will leave you with a better notion of how to approach the subject the next time. And you will have started writing. It's a way to break the ice if you are experiencing a cold spell (not only when you start writing, but at any point in your project).

You need multiple drafts to finish with your best work. By starting early, you give yourself time between drafts. If you read what you have written immediately after writing it, separating the ideas you wanted to convey from the paragraphs you have written may be difficult. As you read, you think not only of what the words convey but also the additional feelings and unarticulated associations that you had in mind. Generally, more time between drafts allows you to get a better perspective on what you have actually said in your writing.

As you revise your early drafts, you can consider changing the order in which your thoughts are presented. You can consider whether some material that has been written in should be excluded and whether any new sections, paragraphs, or sentences should be included. You can check to see if more transition statements ought to be added and whether the transitions that you have already written are clear and helpful to the reader. The paper may be easier both to write and to reorganize if you construct it from notes that you have made on 3 × 5 cards. You can change the order of the cards as you decide on the order in which your points should be made. If you also write the bibliographic information for your sources on these cards (see Chapter 6), your reference citations will be easier to write later.

Make sure you have not plagiarized. Check each of the phrases or ideas you borrowed from other sources to see if you have credited the source. For a direct quotation, use quotation marks and announce the speaker or writer and also the resource from which the quote came, using one of the methods described in Chapter 6. If you paraphrase, tell the reader this, and credit sources in the same way. If you acquired a general idea from another source, you can indicate this in the text of your paper or with a comment note located at the bottom of the page or at the end of the paper.

When you edit for a final draft, check for spelling, grammar, and phrasing. Even if you are good at editing your own paper, you should have at least one other person who is also good at editing read your paper and offer recommendations. You know what you meant in the first place and may tend to see a "correct" reading, overlooking errors that would be obvious to another reader. For the same reason you should have someone else proofread it if possible, checking primarily for typographical errors. Here is a proofreading hint: When proofreading either your own or someone else's writing, start by reading the last word in the paper first, then read the next to the last word, and continue in this direction until you finish at the beginning of the paper. This method prevents the proofreader from seeing what is expected rather than what is on the page.

In its final form the paper is typed or keyed on a computer and double spaced, unless the professor instructs otherwise. It must be done neatly. Ideally, there are no inked or penciled alterations. There should never be many, and they should all be small alterations, such as the insertion of a missing letter in a word. Normally, the left and right margins are one to one and a quarter inches, and the top and bottom margins should be about one inch. Figure 2 displays a standard format for the cover page. Bind the pages of the paper with a paper clip rather than a staple. Plastic or paper binders are often acceptable also.

Writing Style

You wouldn't write a memo like a novel and you wouldn't write a short story like a technical manual. Different kinds of writing have different functions. Your writing style should be adapted to the purpose. It should also reflect the audience you are addressing. You wouldn't write a children's book using the same language that you would use if you were addressing professional anthropologists or attorneys.

When you write a college paper, the primary and sometimes sole reader is the professor of the course for which the paper is written. One common mistake in writing papers is to omit

Figure 2

Love and Suffering in Camus' The Plague

Rennie Medina

Existentialism
Philosophy 37
Westminster College
October 29, 1993

information about a philosopher or philosophical movement because "the professor already knows that." You should explain such things because the professor wants to know whether *you* know the material well enough to characterize it with precision and because your paper should be a topical essay that would have the same persuasive force if read by others. *Write as if you were explaining your topic to an intelligent adult with little or no background in academic philosophy.* Imagine yourself writing for a biologist, psychologist, or computer analyst. Do not condescend and use very simple vocabulary, but do not assume that the reader (even though it may be the professor) knows that you understand the basics of the issue. There are exceptions to this rule. In advanced philosophy courses, you can use philosophical terms like *epistemology* and *metaphysics* with no explanation and even make comparative references to other philosophers, theories, or movements without describing their views.

Some people write very stiffly. That is, their writing sounds awkward because they feel that a paper calls for a rather formal kind of expression, but their version of formality obscures rather than clarifies. Their sentences may be long, with lengthy and confusing clauses. The grammar may be bad because even they get lost in the structure of the sentences they write. They may use words incorrectly and include words they do not normally use and have not mastered. Many of these people speak quite lucidly. If you ask what they meant in one of those unclear phrases, they may be able to tell you straightforwardly and immediately. These people need to write more like they talk. This doesn't mean that everyone should write the way they talk or even that these people should write *exactly* the way they talk. People who have this problem should, however, listen to themselves articulate a point orally in a simple way before committing it to paper. Perhaps the written sentence will require more precision, but listening to the directness of oral expression may be a good start as they try to undo their misconceptions about academic communication.

Other people need the opposite advice. They should try to stop writing the way they talk. Generally, these are people who write in such an informal, everyday colloquial manner that vagueness obscures points and the trendy or folksy flavor of the writing is distracting.

Strive for a paper that is both readable and precise. Say exactly what you mean but say it as clearly as possible. Remember to maintain a tone of open-mindedness, intimating a broad perspective despite the quite specific claims and arguments you make in support of one view.

Word Processing on Computers

Increasing numbers of students are using word processing programs on home computers to write their papers. In some classes, students are required to compose their written work on a computer.

Of the various powerful word processing programs that provide numerous aids for the paper writer, *WordPerfect* and *Microsoft Word* are two of the most popular. There are simpler word processors, but they typically lack many of the special features you may find useful. If you have a paper due soon and you have decided to use a word processor with which you are unfamiliar, spend a day or more learning the basics before you start keying in the paper. Trying to learn the program while you are making content and style decisions can be frustrating. The paper will probably suffer too. Using a word processor with which you are unfamiliar also increases the possibility that you will unintentionally delete material. There are various ways to lose some or all of what you have composed on a computer. Be sure you know how to save the material you are writing. Save often during a writing day, and back up your work by copying the current version of your paper on an extra diskette.

Word processors allow you freedom to reword, add, delete, and edit at the same stage in the writing. You still produce a complete draft, then revise it, and revise it again. But at any point in the development of a single draft, you can easily make any changes that come to mind. The result is usually better writing or less time spent to produce the same quality of writing. You can feel free to use tentative wording that has to be redone, while you go on to the next sentence or paragraph. Your ideas are preserved so you won't forget them, and you don't have to interrupt the flow of your thoughts to develop fully one sentence or phrase at a time. At any point, you can pause and return to work on the tentative wording. Most computer users find that after a little experience they no longer feel the need to begin with a longhand draft. They compose right at the keyboard.

Full-service word processors have many useful features. A spellchecker enables you to identify any words in the document that are not in its built-in lexicon. Of course, this does not enable you to identify problems caused by keyboarding the wrong word. For example, if you mistakenly keyed in "male" instead of "mail," the spellchecker would not alert you to this fact because both are "in the dictionary." (A few programs offer some help in this area by registering the context of surrounding words and telling you when it is likely that the wrong word has been used, but this capability is limited.) In any event, the spellchecker never changes the keyed spelling. It signals a possible misspelling, and waits for you to decide whether you want to change it. If you use a full-service word processor, you can call up a thesaurus that suggests possible synonyms for a highlighted word in the text. Choose only words with which you are familiar to replace the highlighted word because a synonym for that word in one context may not be synonymous in another.

Computers offer other advantages for authors. A copy of a submitted paper is always available for retrieval on a hard or floppy disk. Otherwise, you should retain a photocopy of each paper. Just keeping track of them is a problem for some people. Word processors can also be used to outline, organize and file notes, and create endnotes, bibliographies, and lists of works cited. In addition, computers can access databases and perform other research tasks. (See Chapter 7.)

Students who neither own a home computer nor have access to one owned by a friend or acquaintance may find that the academic library has a learning resources area in which computers are available for student or even public use. Many campuses also have computer labs that are located elsewhere on campus. Advance sign-ups may be permitted (and necessary) to get a time slot in a computer lab. Remember that there are times during the school term in which the demand for computer time will be high. Don't chance it. If you intend to use these computers and reservations are accepted, sign up for the time slots you need as soon as you make your schedule, right after receiving the assignment in class.

5

Language

Being able to say precisely what you mean, orally or in writing, is an important communication skill. Graduates of colleges and universities are expected to display consistent proficiency at it. Language mastery is a basic skill that, added to technical expertise in the field, enables a well-educated person to communicate both established and new ideas in one or more areas of study. Much of higher education focuses on the development of the language skills involved in concept analysis, and this is one of the primary reasons that papers are assigned, critiqued, and graded in college courses.

Precision of Expression

The language and content of written work are not separable. Of course, aspects like spelling and punctuation can be critiqued separately from the ideas themselves. Phrasing and word choice, however, are not separable from meaning. Subtle changes in wording significantly alter the claims that are made. This can then alter the truth of the claims and the evidence needed to support the change. Inattention to wording, or a more basic lack of sensitivity to language, leaves you saying what you don't mean or what you cannot justify. Think about what you mean to say, then say what you mean! You will not have "said" anything except what the words convey.

Overstatement

Writers as well as speakers sometimes make bolder and less supportable claims than they should. They may do this partly because of their zeal for the general idea that they are putting into words. They may also have a habitually sloppy approach to language. Nearly everyone at least occasionally inflates language and exaggerates claims.

In informal everyday dialogue, overstatement is commonplace. "Everyone in the whole school gets along so well," claims a satisfied parent of a public school student. The parent may dismiss a counterexample or two that may be issued in challenge, maintaining that it is really true that "everyone" gets along well. The overstatement may be considered by that parent and by others to be quite acceptable, and the challenger may be thought of as nit-picking. Conversational exaggeration of this sort is frequent and generally harmless.

Habit of overstatement spills over, however, to both informal and formal discussions of politics. A liberal may say that political conservatives "never have any concern about the poor in this country." A conservative may say that liberals "are all irresponsible in dealing with the nation's finances." These broad generalizations, with the words *never* and *all*, invite us to overlook the variety of people who warrant each of these classifications. For good examples of claims that are indefensible because they are not appropriately qualified, we can simply read or listen to some political campaign rhetoric, or read certain newspaper columnists, especially on those hot political and social themes. The habit of overstatement also spills over into our dealings in business and conversations at home. It shows up where it hurts, from job applications to rumor-passing to interactions between professionals of all sorts.

Since most of us have acquired this habit to some extent, it is not surprising that it shows up in the writing of college papers, where precision of expression and rational defense of one's claims are required.

Whether you are wording the thesis itself or constructing a line of argument to support it, choose your words carefully. Don't write "Abortion is the same as murder" if you mean that all abortions are murders or if you mean that abortion fits nearly any general definition of murder. Abortion and murder are *not the same*, after all, since murder has a broader definition. Not all murders are abortions. Don't write "Existentialists do not care about theory" if you mean that most existentialists believe that theorizing rather than reflection that results in action has been the focus of philosophy for too long. You could also then note that much theoretical work was done by those we call existentialists.

Some poorly stated claims, like the preceding one about existentialism, are simple misstatements as much as overstatements.

Vagueness

Your writing is vague when it is too general for your readers. The information or claims are not sufficiently specific. If readers are likely to respond, "But that doesn't tell me enough," then your writing is vague.

Vagueness depends on audience and context. A single description of a disease may be suitable for a layperson's guide to illness, but it may be extremely vague in a pathology article for physicians. Vague answers are often intentional and acceptable in casual conversation. They are sometimes offered in purposeful efforts to avoid giving specific information or to spare someone's feelings. In an academic paper, however, vagueness is seldom appropriate. Thinking of your reader as an intelligent nonphilosopher, or at the most as someone who is familiar with basic philosophical terms and views, you should work on being specific in your writing as you lay out evidence and argument.

There is not a sharp line of demarcation between statements or descriptions that are vague and ones that are not. It is easier to say whether one statement is less vague than another. Since a vague paper is not a well-written one, strive to be specific as consistently as you can. In a paper on the pre-Socratic philosopher Thales, the statement, "Thales believed water to be the basic stuff of the universe," could be made more specific by writing, "Thales believed water to be the source of all other materials in the world." In a paper on Plato, the statement, "The forms were ideas, but not anybody's in particular," could be fashioned into a clearer, more specific one by writing, "The forms were mental entities with an existence independent of any individual thinker." In a paper on the concept of the state of nature in the seventeenth century, the statement, "Hobbes thought everybody always acts selfishly," would be less likely to be misunderstood if it were written, "Hobbes thought that even the cooperative efforts of individuals in society could be explained by their wanting to maintain the security of organized society."

Of course, the statements that were examined and revised in the preceding paragraph might not have required the same sort of revision in the actual paper. Some of the vagueness might have been cleared up in other sentences in the passages from which they were drawn. These sentences were considered out of their context (an entire paper or paragraph) so a point could be made here with several quick examples. Some of the vagueness in the examples, however, was not dependent on the context they might have been set in, and some kind of revision would have been desirable.

Definition

When an important word or phrase in your paper means something different when used by different people, you should define the expression to clarify how *you* are using it. For example, in a paper in which you discuss whether various traditional arguments for the existence of God are sound, you should define "God." Some of the traditional arguments establish at most the existence of a powerful creative entity, not the God that most Christians have in mind. For example, the failure of the first cause argument, the prime mover argument, and the teleological argument to establish the existence of a Christian sort of God is often overlooked. Therefore, it is important to define the term and measure your success according to the definition you have chosen to work with and share with your readers.

Any expressions that may be understood in a way different from the one you intend should be defined if the difference has an effect on whether the evidence and argument offered in the paper are compelling. By "communism" do you mean the political systems that were recently in place in Eastern Europe, the Soviet Union, and China? Or do you mean a theoretical utopia of shared resources that has never been realized on a large scale?

By "self-interest" do you mean egotistical preoccupation with oneself or do you include the prudent advancement of one's own benefit without neglect of others? Terms as basic as "human nature," "idea," "free will," "rights," "essence," "responsibility," "art," "consequences," "substance," and "belief" can be used differently in philosophical systems from the way they are used in everyday discourse. They can also be used differently from one philosophical system to another.

After you have defined an expression, be consistent in your own use of it. Be wary of *equivocation:* this occurs when you shift from one meaning of a term to another without acknowledging the shift, just as if there had been no shift. Equivocation is dangerous because it can create the impression that a conclusion follows from the evidence when it really doesn't. In a paper on free will, "free" may be used in one paragraph to indicate lack of physical restraint, in another paragraph to indicate ability to do anything one wishes, and in the conclusion or thesis it may mean psychological freedom, the possibility of choosing differently in identical circumstances. Observations about freedom that seem to lead to the conclusion may actually rest on different meanings; these observations may only appear to be related to the conclusion if we fail to distinguish between the different meanings of the word.

Grammar

In college, any written work you have prepared at home for submission to the class or the professor is expected to be grammatically correct. This book cannot provide you with the kind of thorough review you can find in one of the standard guides to grammar. However, the following observations will remind you of some basics that should not be violated.

Complete Sentences

Always use complete sentences (with a subject and main verb) except in those rare cases in which you intentionally fashion a sentence fragment for stylistic effect. Conversational patterns of discourse sometimes lead writers to present a partial sentence as if it were a complete sentence.

Wrong: Descartes resolved to doubt everything that was doubtable. Which led him to an extreme, though counterfeit, skepticism in the first *Meditation.*

Right: Descartes resolved to doubt everything that was doubtable, which led him to an extreme, though counterfeit, skepticism in the first *Meditation.*

Also right: Descartes resolved to doubt everything that was doubtable. This led him to an extreme, though counterfeit, skepticism in the first *Meditation.*

The dependent clause that was set off as a separate sentence in the wrong version is joined with the main clause in the first correction and becomes a proper independent sentence in the second correction.

Sometimes two sentences that should be separate are joined into one cumbersome and faulty sentence.

Wrong: Descartes resolved to doubt everything that was doubtable this led him to an extreme, though counterfeit, skepticism in the first Meditation.

Also wrong: Descartes resolved to doubt everything that was doubtable, this led him to an extreme, though counterfeit, skepticism in the first Meditation.

In the first of the two preceding examples, there is no separator to mark off one sentence from the other. In the second example, a comma is used, but it is not a strong enough separator to mark off one complete thought from another. An alternative is to meld the two ideas so they constitute a single thought. For example, you could write: "Descartes' resolve to doubt everything that was doubtable led him to an extreme, though counterfeit, skepticism in the first *Meditation.*"

Agreement Between Parts of a Sentence

The subject and main verb of a sentence must agree in number, and all pronouns should agree in number with their antecedents. In other words, subject and verb as well as pronoun and antecedent should match up, both being singular or both being plural.

The agreement of subject and verb is basic in our sentence structures and usually poses no problem for college students. One tricky case, however, is a sentence with two subjects, one of which is singular while the other is plural, when the subjects are joined by "or" or "nor." Should you use a singular or plural verb form? Generally, the verb form should match the nearer subject.

Wrong: Either the Greek philosopher Pythagoras or the later Pythagoreans was responsible for the now famous Pythagorean theorem.

Right: Either the Greek philosopher Pythagoras or the later Pythagoreans were responsible for the now famous Pythagorean theorem.

Also right: Either the later Pythagoreans or the Greek philosopher Pythagoras himself, their founder, was responsible for the now famous Pythagorean theory.

In the two acceptable forms, the verb is singular or plural to match the nearer subject, the singular "Pythagoras" or the plural "Pythagoreans." Another undesirable form would display a plural verb that is nearer to the subject "Pythagoras."

Confusion can be caused by nouns or pronouns that occur between the subject and verb (that is, by phrases that modify the subject).

Wrong: The complexity of Nietzsche's interwoven themes frustrate some readers.

Right: The complexity of Nietzsche's interwoven themes frustrates some readers.

"Complexity" is singular, so the appropriate verb form is "frustrates." The noun nearer the verb ("themes") is plural, but that is not the subject of the sentence. It is the object of a prepositional phrase.

A pronoun must agree with its antecedent, just as a verb must agree with its subject. If the word to which the pronoun refers is singular, the pronoun must be singular. Otherwise, both are plural.

Wrong: A phenomenologist will apply their philosophical method to a wide range of everyday experiences.

Right: Phenomenologists will apply their philosophical method to a wide range of everyday experiences.

In the first of the two preceding sentences, the plural pronoun "their" is paired with a singular subject. This problem was solved by making the subject plural. Solutions will vary from sentence to sentence.

A pronoun must have an explicit antecedent to which it refers. If the pronoun is the subject of a sentence, its antecedent should have appeared nearby in a previous sentence. If the antecedent precedes its pronoun by several sentences, the reader may lose track. Sometimes authors provide no antecedent at all. This is unacceptable. An author who has been writing about rationalism may use the word "they" to refer to rationalists, although the word "rationalists" has not been used. This is grammatically awkward and incorrect. The passage must be rewritten.

Case

A pronoun's case is the form it takes to display its role in the sentence as a subject, object, or possessor. Subjects take the subjective or nominative case (e.g., I, we, he, she, they, who). Objects of a verb or preposition take the objective case (e.g., me, us, him, her, them, whom). The possessive case shows ownership (e.g., my, our, his, her, their, whose).

Consider the following examples.

Wrong: Kierkegaard and me would not disagree that the ethical level of being is more advanced than the aesthetic.

Right: Kierkegaard and I would not disagree that the ethical level of being is more advanced than the aesthetic.

Wrong: John Wisdom and her are the only philosophers to approach language in that way.

Right: John Wisdom and she are the only philosophers to approach language in that way.

Wrong: The tutor sharply criticized Devon and I.

Right: The tutor sharply criticized Devon and me.

Wrong: Strawson is a better writer than him.

Right: Strawson is a better writer than he.

For the Kierkegaard examples, confirm the correct usage by mentally leaving out the first two words of each of the two sentences. Leave out the words "Kierkegaard and." You wouldn't begin a sentence by writing "Me would not disagree." You would begin with "I would not disagree." In compound subjects and objects, you can test your usage by keeping the pronoun and leaving out the other item. The correct pronoun is then usually obvious. The John Wisdom examples can be tested in the same way, although you have to change the plural verb to a singular one. You would not begin a sentence by writing "Her is the only philosopher." You would begin with "She is the only philosopher." Again, in the next set of examples, the same test can be applied. Would you write or say "The tutor sharply criticized I," or would you use the word "me"? The correctness of the second version becomes clear. Finally, the Strawson examples can be understood if you realize that an unstated "is" follows the last word of the sentence. We wouldn't say "than him is." We would say "than he is."

Misplaced Sentence Parts

Words or phrases are sometimes inserted in sentences at places where they simply do not fit. The results are awkward sentence structures and unnecessary sacrifice of a comfortable flow of wording for the reader. The bottom line is that the writing becomes less clear.

In some cases, entire phrases are misplaced. Consider this sentence.

J. L. Austin examines the concept of responsibility in his essay, *A Plea for Excuses,* which is very important in moral philosophy.

The author of this sentence meant that the concept of responsibility is very important in moral philosophy. However, the modifying phrase "which is very important in moral philosophy" was placed immediately after the title of the essay. This placement gives many readers the impression that the essay is very important in moral philosophy. Other readers may discern the ambiguity and be uncertain about the author's intention. The author would have avoided confusion by writing:

> J. L. Austin examines the concept of responsibility, which is very important in moral philosophy, in his essay, *A Plea for Excuses*.

The rewording moves the dangling modifier (the "which is" phrase) so it is beside the word it modifies. This is a common solution for a common problem.

In other cases, moving a single word can make a big difference in the message that you convey. Notice what happens when the word *only* is placed differently in otherwise identical sentences. Although the word "fits" in each case, the meaning changes completely.

> Professor Wu claimed that Socrates only wrote poetry.
> *Meaning: She claimed that Socrates wrote nothing besides poetry.*

> Professor Wu claimed that only Socrates wrote poetry.
> *Meaning: She claimed that no one else wrote poetry!*

> Professor Wu claimed only that Socrates wrote poetry.
> *Meaning: She claimed nothing else.*

> Only Professor Wu claimed that Socrates wrote poetry.
> *Meaning: No one else claimed it.*

Parallelism

Words, phrases, or sentences presented in series should be in parallel form. That is, multiple items presented as if they are on one level should share the same grammatical structure. Here is an example. The first sentence does not display parallel construction. The second corrects the error.

> ***Wrong:*** Wittgenstein wrote *Tractatus Logico-Philosophicus*, was the author of *Philosophical Investigations*, writing also "A Lecture on Ethics."

> ***Right:*** Wittgenstein wrote *Tractatus Logico-Philosophicus*, *Philosophical Investigations*, and "A Lecture on Ethics."

Here the problem of having unparallel items in a series is solved by using one introductory verb and linking the items with commas. Sometimes different verbs must be used with various items in the series. An example follows.

Wrong: The pre-Socratic philosophers of ancient Greece wondered at the complexity of the world, had looked for a principle of unity in all the diversity, and claiming a principle of permanence in a sea of change.

Right: The pre-Socratic philosophers of ancient Greece wondered at the complexity of the world, looked for a principle of unity in all the diversity, and claimed a principle of permanence in a sea of change.

In this case, a different verb is part of each item in the series. In the corrected version, each verb has the same form. Here it is the preterit tense.

Lists sometimes display unparallel structure. Consider two versions of the same list:

Wrong: What do philosophers do? Their activities are diverse. Philosophers may be found doing the following sorts of things:
(a) writing papers for publication in professional journals
(b) teaching college classes
(c) internships and residencies in prisons, schools, and even art museums
(d) they are on ethics committees in hospitals
(e) writing books for scholars
(f) books for the public are sometimes written by philosophers
(g) consulting for business and industry
(h) serving on government task forces and committees.

Right: What do philosophers do? Their activities are diverse. Philosophers may be found doing the following sorts of things:
(a) writing papers for publication in professional journals
(b) teaching college classes
(c) serving internships and residencies in prisons, schools, and even art museums
(d) serving on ethics committees in hospitals
(e) writing books for scholars
(f) writing books for the public
(g) consulting for business and industry
(h) serving on government task forces and committees.

In the corrected version, parallel structure has been achieved by rewriting several of the items. An appropriate form for the items can be determined by reviewing the wording of the introductory passage. Here gerunds serve the purpose well. Often, the initial items in a series will take an appropriate form. Then you will forget how the introductory passage was worded and start creating various forms for later items. If you make this mistake, you should at least notice it when it is time to revise and edit the draft.

Punctuation

Professors also expect correct punctuation. All punctuation marks have been misused at one time or another. Some kinds of misuse are common. The most common ones are noted here.

A **comma** should not be used to separate two complete thoughts—that is, two independent clauses. The result is one form of a "run-on" sentence.

> *Wrong:* Quine and Ullian wrote *The Web of Belief*, it has an especially well-written chapter on hypotheses.

> *Right:* Quine and Ullian wrote *The Web of Belief*. It has an especially well-written chapter on hypotheses.

> *Another solution:* Quine and Ullian's *The Web of Belief* has an especially well-written chapter on hypotheses.

The comma does not provide a sufficiently strong separation between the two independent clauses in the original example. Each is capable of standing alone. The first solution is acceptable, but the second solution flows better and is more concise. Another misuse of the comma is its placement within a main clause where it is unnecessary.

> *Wrong:* William James's books are read, in both philosophy and psychology classes.

> *Right:* William James's books are read in both philosophy and psychology classes.

There is no need to set off the prepositional phrase with commas. Short sentences like these seldom require a comma, except after an introductory word like "however" or "instead." The most basic of the several rules on avoiding incorrect comma placement is: Do not use a comma to separate the subject from its verb, the verb from its object, or an adjective from its noun.

Colons and **semicolons** are frequently misused and sometimes one is incorrectly used in place of the other. A colon follows an introductory phrase that directs attention to what follows (after the colon). The writer should be wary of overuse of this symbol. A semicolon separates two main clauses that could stand alone as sentences. The semicolon is used instead of a period to show a special relation between those two statements. Each illuminates the other. Semicolons have an additional use. They may be used to separate items in a series when a comma does not provide a sufficiently strong break because the items in the series are long or because they contain commas within themselves.

> *Wrong:* The continental rationalists of the seventeenth century believed that humans will avoid error if they initiate a line of reasoning with clear and distinct ideas; and deduce their logical implications.

> *Right:* The continental rationalists of the seventeenth century believed that humans will avoid error if they initiate a line of reasoning with clear and distinct ideas and deduce their logical implications.

> *Right:* The continental rationalists of the seventeenth century believed that humans will avoid error if they initiate a line of reasoning with clear and distinct ideas and deduce their logical implications; they imagined that the patterns of the mind and the patterns of nature reflected one another.

The most common error involving semicolons is incorrect placement between two unequal parts of a sentence, when one is a main clause that can stand alone as a sentence, but the other is not. This error is illustrated in the first of the three preceding examples (the one labeled *Wrong*). What follows the semicolon in that sentence cannot stand independently as a sentence. "And deduce their logical implications" is not a complete thought with subject and main verb. In the correction below that example, the semicolon is omitted. Below that, another example displays the correct use of a semicolon. Two main clauses that express related thoughts are joined by the semicolon.

An **apostrophe** shows possession or a contraction of two words. To show possession in the singular, you generally place

an apostrophe at the end of the word and add *s*. To show possession in the plural, you generally place an apostrophe after the
plural form of the noun, and you sometimes add *s* to that. The
phrase "the empiricist's assumptions" refers to assumptions of
one empiricist (who perhaps represents others). The phrase "the
empiricists' assumptions" refers to assumptions of more than
one empiricist (and possibly all empiricists). When an apostrophe is used to signal the contraction of two words into one, the
apostrophe is placed where a letter has been omitted. We write
"doesn't" rather than "doe'snt" because the *o* from the word *not*
is omitted. Note an interesting case: *it's* is a contraction of *it is*
(with the apostrophe marking the deleted *i*), leaving the possessive *its* to be spelled without an apostrophe, even though possession is also usually indicated with an apostrophe.

Finally, consider **quotation marks.** When you quote a passage word for word, use quotation marks before and after the
borrowed words. However, when you write to convey the general sense of what was written or said, do not use quotation
marks.

> *Wrong:* Karl Jaspers wrote that "we do not understand our own so-
> ciety because of its complexity and commotion." [The words in
> quotes are not Jaspers' own words.]

> *Right:* Karl Jaspers wrote that we do not understand our own soci-
> ety because of its complexity and commotion. [The words that de-
> scribe his comments are not Jaspers' own words.]

> *Right:* Karl Jaspers wrote, "Owing to the turmoil of modern life,
> what is really happening eludes our comprehension." [The words
> are the author's own or an English translation of them.]

In the first example, a reader might suspect the incorrect use of
quotation marks because of the word *that*. However, if that word
had not been included, the reader would be even more likely to
believe that you were reporting an exact quote.

Sometimes you may want to leave out some words within a
quoted passage. This is permissible if you don't misrepresent the
original meaning and if you use an **ellipsis** mark of three spaced
periods to indicate where the words were omitted. For example,
you might want to quote part of the first sentence in the second
paragraph of John Stuart Mill's *On Liberty*. Consider the whole

sentence: "The struggle between liberty and authority is the most conspicuous feature in the portions of history with which we are earliest familiar, particularly in that of Greece, Rome, and England." The point as it relates to the paper in which the borrowed quotation will appear might be made more effectively if the middle part of the sentence is left out. This is acceptable, but the deletion must be reported to the reader. The result should look like this: "The struggle between liberty and authority is the most conspicuous feature in . . . Greece, Rome, and England."

Gender

Some previously accepted uses of language should be avoided because of the gender inequities they imply. Use of the masculine pronoun in reference to groups that include males and females, for example, is not appropriate and is no longer proper.

> *Wrong:* A utilitarian has to be able to anticipate the actions of people he has never met in order to draw conclusions about the morally right course of action.

> *Wrong:* A utilitarian has to be able to anticipate the actions of people they have never met in order to draw conclusions about the morally right course of action.

> *Right:* A utilitarian has to be able to anticipate the actions of people he or she has never met in order to draw conclusions about the morally right course of action.

> *Right:* Utilitarians have to be able to anticipate the actions of people they have never met in order to draw conclusions about the morally right course of action.

The first example displays the use of a masculine pronoun, *he*, to refer to male and female utilitarians. Avoid this old usage. A common attempt to resolve this difficulty is displayed in the second example. This approach to the problem is not acceptable, since we now have a plural pronoun, *they*, referring to a subject that is grammatically singular (although it is meant to refer to all utilitarians). The third example is grammatically correct, but the "he or she" phrase can be awkward, especially when it recurs frequently. The best solution is shown in the last example. The plural subject is referred to by a plural pronoun. This kind of solution is not always the best one. Solutions vary from case to case. Sometimes creative rewording of the sentence avoids the difficulty.

Replace the generic *man* with *humanity*. Pronoun references to the term are plural, so you could refer back to it with *they* instead of *his*. Also, replace *mankind* with *humankind*.

Finally, some philosophical issues are related to religious topics. Consider the question of gender identity before choosing a pronoun to refer to a divine being.

Spelling

Spelling should be correct on all writing assignments that are prepared out of the classroom. Computer spellcheckers are helpful but not foolproof. Moreover, the responsibility for correct spelling is yours, whether or not you have employed spellcheckers and proofreaders.

Commonly Misspelled Words in Philosophy

Any list of commonly misspelled words for the English language is either very lengthy or highly selective. Let's narrow the scope. A list of commonly misspelled words in philosophy follows. Some readers will recognize a few that they regularly misspell.

> aesthetic (in another correct spelling, the initial a is omitted)
>
> analytic
>
> anarchy
>
> argument (the u is not followed by an e)
>
> atheist
>
> causal (not to be confused with the word *casual*)
>
> coherence
>
> conceive
>
> deceive

deism

deontological

dialectical

dialogue

dualism

effect (often confused with affect)

empirical

empiricism

epiphenomenalism

existence (an e rather than an a follows the t)

existentialism

fallacy

medieval

necessary

ontological

perceive

phenomenology

philosophical

premise

scholasticism

skepticism

solipsism

tautology

teleological

theism

theory

utilitarian

Plurals of Philosophical Terms

Several words that are commonly used in philosophical discourse have plural forms about which many people are unclear. Here is a short list.

Singular	Plural
criterion	criteria
hypothesis	hypotheses
phenomenon	phenomena
schema	schemata
stratum	strata
thesis	theses

Hypothesis, schema, and *thesis* have plural forms with which many people are not familiar or comfortable. The other three words on the list—*criterion, phenomenon,* and *stratum*—demand attention because of the frequency with which people use the plural form when they intend a singular meaning. By grammatical definition, there is *never* one criteria, phenomena, or strata.

6

References to Other Sources

You must acknowledge all the sources you use in developing a paper. Mentioning the name of the author of the source or even giving the title of a book or article is not enough. The reader should be able to look up the acknowledged sources, recreating the original research process. So it is your duty is to give complete publication information. All this detailed information about sources can be included in the text of the paper itself. Among the disadvantages of this approach is the interruption of the flow of ideas that develop the themes of the paper. Scholars have developed the practice of listing sources at the end of a paper and identifying specific references throughout the paper. No single method of doing this has been accepted by all the world's scholars, but a few approaches have become professional standards. Some scholarly disciplines have their own formats.

Most college writing follows one of two basic systems. In one system, notes are placed at the bottom of the pages of the paper (footnotes) after having been signaled in the text by asterisks or superscript numbers. In the other system, parentheses in the text enclose a reference to an author from the list of works cited and designate the page numbers in the work. Each of these systems and the rules for arranging the information are explained in this chapter.

Bibliography

A bibliography at the end of the paper lists the sources used in the development of the paper. From the ancient Greek, the word *bibliography* almost literally means "write down the books." In a modern bibliography, books are nearly always the most numerous sources. However, you may also include articles and nonprint sources.

Some bibliographies list only works cited. Others include works consulted but not referred to in the paper. The bibliography may also be titled "Works Cited" or "Works Consulted."

Add the bibliography to the end of the paper. It should have a page number for each of its pages, continuing the pagination of the paper itself. If the closing paragraph of the paper ends on page 12, the bibliography should begin on page 13. Short papers often have a bibliography that consists of only one page.

The works cited should be listed alphabetically by the authors' last names. When no author is indicated for a work, use the title of the work and enter it alphabetically into the list that is otherwise ordered by author. When alphabetizing a title, ignore the opening word if it is a definite or indefinite article: *The, A,* or *An.* However, include that word as you write the title in the entry.

Citing Books

A bibliographic entry has three major elements: (1) author's name, (2) title of the work, and (3) publication information. Sometimes additional information is required. This depends on the type of publication, as you will discover in this chapter.

The kind of source being cited determines the form of the entry. Citing books is somewhat different from citing articles, other printed matter, and nonprint material such as films and broadcasts.

In book citations, the information is usually arranged in the following order, although not all of these elements are always applicable:

1. Author's name: Last name, comma, first name, period. (To include a second author, replace the period with a comma

and then add the second author without reversing first and last names.)

2. Title: Full title italicized or underlined, period. If there is a subtitle, write main title, colon, subtitle. (If only one specialized part of the book has been used, e.g., a preface or an appendix, give that title, then a period, then the book title.)

3. Editor or translator's name: First name, then last name, preceded by *Ed.* or *Trans.* and followed by a period.

4. Edition: 2nd ed., 3rd ed., etc. (First editions do not require this entry.)

5. Volume number: *Vol. 2.* if only volume 2 of a multivolume work was used. *5 Vols.* if the work has five volumes and more than one was used.

6. Series name: e.g., *Foundations of Philosophy Series.* For a titled series of books. (Most books are not part of a series.)

7. Publisher: City in which published (and the state, if there is any question about it), colon, publishing company, comma, year of publication, e.g., *New York: Norton, 1993.* (All this is available on the opening pages of the book. If more than one city is identified, use the first.)

8. Page numbers: Listing of a specialized part of the book, e.g., appendix, preface, article, if only that part was used. (This part of an entry is seldom necessary.)

The first line of each entry should be flush with the left margin. Any additional lines for that entry should be indented several spaces, with the result that the first line hangs out over the rest on the left side. Double space all entries. Here are some sample bibliographic entries for books.

A book by one author

Ingram, David. <u>Critical Theory and Philosophy.</u> New York:

Paragon, 1990.

Nussbaum, Martha C. <u>The Fragility of Goodness.</u> Cambridge:

Cambridge University Press, 1986.

A book with co-authors

Brickhouse, Thomas C. and Nicholas D. Smith. <u>Socrates on</u>

<u>Trial.</u> Princeton: Princeton University Press, 1990.

Smart, J. J. C. and Bernard Williams. <u>Utilitarianism: For and</u>

<u>Against.</u> Cambridge: Cambridge University Press, 1973.

An anthology of collected work

Kittay, Eva Feder and Diana T. Meyers, eds. <u>Women and Moral</u>

<u>Theory.</u> Savage, MD: Rowman & Littlefield, 1987.

McMullin, Ernan, ed. <u>The Concept of Matter in Greek and</u>

<u>Medieval Philosophy.</u> Notre Dame: University of Notre

Dame Press, 1963.

An article in an anthology

Lee, Edward N. "Reason and Rotation: Circular Movement as

the Model of Mind (Nous) in the Later Plato." <u>Facets of</u>

<u>Plato's Philosophy.</u> Ed. W. H. Werkmeister. Assen: Van

Gorcum, 1976. 70–102.

Russell, Bertrand. "Logical Atomism." <u>Logical Positivism.</u>

Ed. A. J. Ayer. New York: Free Press, 1959. 31–50.

A book with an author and an editor

Hume, David. <u>An Inquiry Concerning Human Understanding.</u>

Ed. Charles W. Hendel. Indianapolis: Bobbs-Merrill, 1955.

Mill, John Stuart. <u>The Subjection of Women.</u> Ed. Susan Moller

    Okin. Indianapolis: Hackett, 1988.

A book with a translator

Camus, Albert. <u>The Stranger.</u> Trans. Stuart Gilbert. New York:

    Vintage, 1946.

Kant, Immanuel. <u>Critique of Pure Reason.</u> Trans. Norman Kemp

    Smith. New York: St. Martin's, 1933.

A multivolume work

Guthrie, W. K. C. <u>The Earlier Presocratics and the</u>

    <u>Pythagoreans.</u> Cambridge: Cambridge University Press,

    1962. Vol. 1 of A History of Greek Philosophy. 6 vols.

    1962–1981.

Jaspers, Karl. <u>Philosophy.</u> Trans. E. B. Ashton. 3 vols. Chicago:

    University of Chicago Press, 1969–1971.

A book in a series

Walsh, James J. and Henry L. Shapiro, eds. <u>Aristotle's Ethics:</u>

    <u>Issues and Interpretations.</u> Wadsworth Studies in

    Philosophical Criticism. Ed. Alexander Sesonske. Belmont,

    CA: Wadsworth, 1967.

Wittgenstein, Ludwig. <u>Tractatus Logico-Philosophicus.</u> Trans.

    D. F. Pears and B. F. McGuinness. International Library of

    Philosophy and Scientific Method. New York: Routledge &

    Kegan Paul, 1960.

A book in another language

Herodotus. <u>Herodoti Historiae</u> [<u>Herodotus's Histories</u>]. Carolus

Hude, ed. 3rd ed. Oxford: Clarendon, 1927.

Unamuno, Miguel de. <u>El Espejo de la Muerte</u> [<u>The Mirror of</u>

<u>Death</u>]. 7th ed. Colección Austral. Madrid: Espasa-Calpe,

1941.

An introduction, preface, foreword, afterword, or appendix

Husserl, Edmund. Author's Preface to the English Edition.

<u>Ideas: General Introduction to Pure Phenomenology.</u> By

Husserl. Trans. W. R. Gibson. New York: Collier, 1962.

5–22.

Koestenbaum, Peter. Introductory essay. <u>The Paris Lectures.</u> By

Edmund Husserl. The Hague: Martinus Nijhoff, 1970.

ix–lxxvii.

An article in a reference work

"Logos." <u>Greek Philosophical Terms: A Historical Lexicon.</u> F. E.

Peters. New York: New York University Press, 1967.

Warnock, G. J. "Reason." <u>Encyclopedia of Philosophy.</u> 1967 ed.

Citing Articles in Periodicals

Periodicals are issued "periodically." They are publications that
are published in issues that are brought out at regular intervals,
e.g., weekly or monthly. Philosophy papers that focus on academic philosophical themes usually cite more scholarly journals
than other kinds of periodicals. These contain articles that are
written by professional philosophers and directed to their colleagues. Philosophy papers on general themes such as practical

ethics or public policy may have more magazine and newspaper citations.

A bibliographic entry for a periodical has the same three major elements as an entry for a book: (1) author's name, (2) title of the work, and (3) publication information. In periodical citations, the information is usually arranged in the following order:

1. Author's name: Same form of entry as that for books.
2. Title: Enclosed within quotation marks. Period precedes closing quotation mark.
3. Name of periodical: Italicized or underlined, period.
4. Series, volume, and issue number: Only for journals, though most have no series number. Close with period. (A special series is sometimes identified with a name instead of a number.)
5. Publication date and page numbers: For journals, year of publication in parentheses, colon, page numbers of article. For other periodicals, date without parentheses, edition (if any), colon, page numbers, period.

Here are some sample bibliographic entries for periodicals.

A magazine article

Church, George J. "Splinter, Splinter Little State." <u>Time</u> 6 July

1992: 36–39.

Kinoshita, June. "Dreams of a Rat." <u>Discover</u> July 1992:

34–41.

A newspaper article

Hoyle, Martin. "Dazzling Journey into Moral Maze." <u>Times</u>

[London] 8 June 1992, arts: 2.

Ollman, Leah. "New Visions of Public Art in San Diego." <u>Los</u>

<u>Angeles Times</u> 1 July 1992, San Diego edition: F1.

A scholarly journal

Journals have a volume number for a set of issues (called numbers). Volume 12 of a journal may be issued in four issues/numbers. The second issue of volume 12 is designated in the bibliographic entry like this: *12.1*. If each issue begins with page one, you must give volume and issue number. If the journal paginates continuously from one issue of a volume number to another (e.g., issue 2 may begin on page 165), you may omit the issue number and the month or season of publication.

Journals publish reviews of books in the field as well as original articles. *Rev. of* stands for "review of." Also note that the Gale entry that follows refers to a monograph series in which a single paper is published in each issue, so page numbers are unnecessary. Finally, when there are two or more consecutive entries for the same author, all entries subsequent to the first show ————. where the name would otherwise be located (at the beginning of the entry). See the Vlastos entries in this list.

Bailin, Sharon. "Critical and Creative Thinking." Informal Logic 9 (1987): 23–30.

Flax, Neil M. Rev. of Positions by Jacques Derrida. Philosophy and Literature 5 (1981): 237–38.

Gale, Richard. "Negation and Non-Being." American Philosophical Quarterly monograph series 10 (1976).

Gracia, Jorge J. E. "Texts and Their Interpretation." Review of Metaphysics 43 (1990): 495–542.

Hayry, Matti and Heta Hayry. "AIDS in a Small North European Country—A Study in Applied Ethics." International Journal of Applied Philosophy 3.3 (Spring 1987): 51–61.

Herman, Barbara. "Mutual Aid and Respect for Persons."

    Ethics 94 (1984): 577–602.

Ketchum, Sara Ann and Christine Pierce. "Rights and

    Responsibilities." Journal of Medicine and Philosophy 6

    (1981): 271–79.

Monserrate, Jaime E. Toro. "De Wittgenstein a la filosofia de la

    accion." Dialogos 17.39 (Apr. 1982): 71–80.

Prasad, Rajendra. "The Concept of Moksa." Philosophy and

    Phenomenological Research 31 (1971): 381–93.

Stough, Charlotte L. "Forms and Explanation in the 'Phaedo.'"

    Phronesis 21.1 (1976): 1–30.

Vlastos, Gregory. "Is the 'Socratic Fallacy' Socratic?" Ancient

    Philosophy 10 (1990): 1–16.

———. "Reasons and Causes in the 'Phaedo.'" Philosophical

    Review 78 (1969): 291–325.

To decide how to create an entry for an unusual printed re-source or for nonprint resources, consult the *MLA Handbook for Writers of Research Papers*, third edition, by Joseph Gibaldi and Walter S. Achtert (New York: Modern Language Association, 1988).

Documentation with Footnotes or Endnotes

For many people, the most familiar form of documentation for specific passages in a paper is the use of notes—footnotes or endnotes. Footnotes are located at the bottom of the page on which the reference is cited. Endnotes appear at the end of the paper. Notes are signaled in the text of the paper by a super-script number, raised above the line of type at the end of the passage that requires the reference. Since the information in a reference note is similar to the information in a bibliographic entry, bibliographies are sometimes omitted when notes are used. Still, many professors expect both.

Reference notes have four elements: (1) author's name, (2) title of the work, (3) publication information, and (4) page reference.

Citing Books: First Reference

The initial note referring to each book takes a standard form that provides full identification of the book. Subsequent references to the same book are much briefer, and will be discussed later in this chapter.

A book by one author

[1]Mary Whitlock Blundell, <u>Helping Friends and Harming Enemies: A Study in Sophocles and Greek Ethics</u> (Cambridge: Cambridge University Press, 1989) 207.

A book with co-authors

[2]Schuyler W. Huck and Howard M. Sandler, <u>Rival Hypotheses: Alternative Interpretations of Data Based Conclusions</u> (New York: Harper & Row, 1979) 11, 158.

An anthology of collected work

[3]F. S. C. Northrop and Mason W. Gross, <u>Alfred North Whitehead: An Anthology</u> (New York: Macmillan, 1961) 9.

An article in an anthology

[4]Julius Moravcsik, "Learning as Recollection," <u>Plato,</u> ed. Gregory Vlastos, vol. 1 (Garden City: Anchor-Doubleday, 1971) 54–55.

A book with an author, a translator, and an editor

[5]Gottfried Wilhelm von Leibniz, Leibniz: Discourse on Metaphysics, Correspondence with Arnauld, and Monadology, trans. George R. Montgomery, ed. Eugene Freeman (LaSalle: Open Court, 1968) 28.

A multivolume work

[6]Frederick Copleston, A History of Philosophy, vol. 8 part 2 (Garden City: Image-Doubleday, 1967) 199–205.

A book in a series

[7]Thomas S. Kuhn, The Structure of Scientific Revolutions, International Encyclopedia of Unified Science ser 2.2 (Chicago: University of Chicago Press, 1962) 35–36.

A book in another language

[8]Hermann Gundert, Dialog und Dialektik: Zur Struktur des platonischen Dialogs [Dialogue and Dialectic: On the Structure of the Platonic Dialogues] (Amsterdam: Verlag B. R. Gruner N. V., 1971) 48.

An introduction, preface, foreword, afterword, or appendix

[9]Martin Ostwald, translator's introduction, Nicomachean Ethics by Aristotle (Indianapolis: Bobbs-Merrill, 1962) xxii.

An article in a reference work

[10]"Alcibiades," Who Was Who in the Greek World, 1984 ed.

Citing Articles: First Reference

A magazine article

[11]Don S. Rice and Prudence M. Rice, "Collapse to Contact: Postclassic Archaeology of the Peten Maya," Archaeology Mar.– Apr. 1984: 46–51.

A newspaper article

[12]Ellen K. Coughlin, "New Access to Scrolls is Unlikely to Settle Scholarly Dispute," Chronicle of Higher Education 6 November 1991: A9.

A scholarly journal

[13]Anne Boykin and Savina O. Schoenhofer, "Story as Link Between Nursing Practice, Ontology, Epistemology," Image: Journal of Nursing Scholarship 23 (1991): 245–246.

[14]Joyce Trebilcot, "Sex Roles: The Argument from Nature," Ethics 85 (1975) 250.

[15]Sanford Pinsker, "Revisionist Thought, Academic Power, and the Aging American Intellectual," The Gettysburg Review 3 (1990): 420.

[16]Jorge J. E. Gracia, "Philosophical Analysis in Latin America," History of Philosophy Quarterly 1 (1984): 112.

[17]Annette Baier, "Mixing Memory and Desire," American Philosophical Quarterly 13 (1976): 213–214.

Second and Subsequent References to Books and Articles

After the first reference, the notes are easy to write. The last name of the author or authors, followed by the page number for the new reference, is sufficient. Here are some examples:

[18]Baier 220.

[19]Boykin and Schoenhofer 247.

[20]Trebilcot 251.

If more than one work by a single author or by co-authors has already been cited, you must be specific enough in your second reference to identify the correct source. Usually a key word of phrase from the title will serve the purpose. Here is an example:

[21]Kant, Prolegomena 50–51.

[22]Kant, Pure Reason 107, 113.

The first of the two Kant references is to his *Prolegomena to any Future Metaphysics.* The second reference is to his *Critique of Pure Reason.* If you make a second reference to this "Critique," you may use the entire title, *Critique of Pure Reason* instead of the abbreviation in the preceding reference. However, you may want to avoid the abbreviation *Critique* since Kant also published the *Critique of Practical Reason* and the *Critique of Judgment.* Certainly, if either of these two other titles had been referenced earlier in the same paper, the abbreviation *Critique* is an inappropriate choice.

Commentary Notes

Notes at the foot of a page or at the end of the paper may also be used for commentary by the author when the remarks are a sidelight to the development of the ideas in the paper or would disrupt the flow of those ideas. The notes may be short or long.

Charlotte L. Stough, in her previously referred to article in the journal *Phronesis* (21.1), employs many of these commentary notes. Here is one of them:

[39]My argument in this section has been a negative one. It has not been my intention to offer a detailed interpretation of the text from 103 d to the end of the immortality argument. That complicated passage raises more questions than I could hope to deal with in this paper. Instead I have focused on a single problem which bears directly on my thesis with the aim of showing that nothing in Plato's language there commits him to a tripartite ontology. Given these limitations of objective, the thesis set forth in this paper will be compatible with more than one interpretation of that passage.

In many of Stough's notes, she combines commentary and reference to another work. Her forty-second note is an example of this:

[42]My conclusion in its most general form thus accords with Paul Shorey's contention that in the Phaedo Plato "is really describing a possible procedure of logic and not a false a priori method of the investigation of nature" ("The Origin of the Syllogism," Classical Philology 19 (1924) 8).

Stough's last note, placed at the very end of the last paragraph of her paper, is used to acknowledge support:

[44]Most of the work for this paper was done while I held a fellowship at the Center for Hellenic Studies in Washington,

D. C., which I gratefully acknowledge. A similar version of the paper was presented at the December, 1973 meeting of the Society for Ancient Greek Philosophy in Atlanta, Georgia.

Students in philosophy classes may augment their papers with commentary notes for clarification or additional observation, but they should not use them for personal remarks about their preparation or understanding of the material or assignment. Here is a sample of a student's commentary note:

[22]The expression "critically analyze" is used here to describe a process in which a person attempts to discern (1) the intention of the original author, as well as (2) strengths and weaknesses in that author's reasoning.

This definition of an important expression might be included in the body of the student's paper. The student must decide whether placement in the main text or a commentary note is more appropriate.

Parenthetical Documentation

The Modern Language Association of America, known as the MLA, has refined a system of parenthetical documentation. With this system, documentary notes—footnotes or endnotes—are unnecessary. The bibliography, now known as the list of "works cited," gives author, title, and publishing information for each work cited. Consequently, the only thing required is a way to flag the correct entry for readers as they progress through the paper—and a specific page number each time such a reference is made. With this system, the only notes that remain are the commentary notes with special remarks for the reader.

In a paper, parenthetical documentation should be placed wherever a reference is made to one of the works cited. Usually only the page number or numbers of the cited passage need to be put in parentheses. If more information is necessary for clarity, add it. Additional information may include the author's name, the title, the volume number, of the name of a section of the book.

To refer to an entire work, without specific focus on a certain part or passage, simply use the author's name. Do not use only a title; the works cited are listed by author. A reader's quick check for the entry will be easier if you identify the author. If the author is not mentioned in the sentence that requires acknowledgment, place the author's name in parentheses. If the author has more than one work cited on the list, then write a short form of the title in parentheses.

Dewey placed the work of art in the human psyche and distinguished between active and passive phases in the aesthetic consciousness. [One work by Dewey listed in Works Cited]

On the other hand, the work of art has been placed, through definition, in the human psyche (Dewey) rather than in the object. [One work by Dewey listed in Works Cited; Dewey not named in sentence]

Despite his taste for writing novels and plays, Sartre was also capable of philosophical system-building (Being). [More than one work by Sartre listed in Works Cited]

To refer to certain pages or a specific part of a work (e.g., introduction), place the page number(s) or part name in parentheses. If the author has not been named, precede the page number with the author's name. If more than one work by the author is on the list of works cited, name the work before giving the page number and enclose them together in parentheses.

Tillich distinguishes between symbols and signs (41–43). [One work by Tillich listed in Works Cited]

It is not a recent insight that "it is a common failing of mortals to deem the more difficult the fairer" (Descartes 29). [One work by Descartes listed in Works Cited]

It is not a recent insight that "it is a common failing of mortals to deem the more difficult the fairer" (Descartes, Rules 29). [More than one work by Descartes listed in Works Cited]

Descartes observed that "it is a common failing of mortals to deem the more difficult the fairer" (Rules 29). [More than one work by Descartes listed in Works Cited; Descartes named in sentence]

For a multivolume work, the volume number and a colon should precede the page number.

Leibniz's work was not well known by Berkeley (Matson 2: 347). [One work by Matson listed in Works Cited; Matson not named in sentence]

Matson claims that Leibniz's work was not well known by Berkeley (2:347). [One work by Matson listed in Works Cited; Matson named in sentence]

An exact quote or a paraphrase that is derived from a secondary source may be cited, but the symbol *qtd. in* must be used in the parenthetical documentation. Even vague reference to the quoted material may be made in this way.

Julian Huxley claimed that the mind-body problem must be approached from what he called "the evolutionary angle" (qtd. in Russell 3:249).

It is also possible to refer to two sources in one parenthetical reference. Simply separate the two with a semicolon.

Theophrastus, in writing the history of the presocratics, assimilated the biases of Aristotle rather than assessing the evidence freshly, with the possibility of coming to original conclusions (Allen 26–27; Kirk and Raven 3–4).

Again, for documentation rules that cover cases not examined here, consult the *MLA Handbook for Writers of Research Papers*.

Other Systems of Documentation

The number system of documentation is a variety of parenthetical documentation. The listings in Works Cited are numbered in series. The entries may be ordered alphabetically, chronologically, or according to any other plan. In each set of documentary parentheses, the number of the work is cited instead of the author's name. The number, sometimes underlined, is followed by a comma and the page number.

In another system, called in-text citation, the person who writes the paper provides all reference information in the body of the paper. Neither a list of works cited nor documentary notes are used. Papers with very few references are the most likely candidates for this method. The form is basically bibliographic, but commas replace periods.

Philip Rahv, in his introduction to <u>Selected Stories of Franz Kafka</u> (New York: Modern-Random, 1952), identifies <u>In the Penal Colony</u> as a transition between the early works in which the principle of authority has the form of a familial father and the later works in which that principle has been "generalized into an institutional power."

With a Socratic lament for those who give up the fight to develop a strong moral character, Marcus Aurelius wrote, "It is a shame when the soul is first to give way in this life, and the body does not give way" (<u>Meditations,</u> Roslyn, NY: Walter J. Black, 1945).

7

Research

Most topics for philosophy papers require research. The customary ways to acknowledge research sources are described in Chapter 6. In Chapter 7, the activity of researching is explored. First, general library skills are described: how to find books, periodicals, and other resources that illuminate a selected topic. Then, philosophical resources are featured. In these sections of the chapter, special volumes on philosophy as well as philosophical journals and the Philosopher's Index are examined.

Library Skills

A library—public, private, or academic—is an extremely useful resource for a literate person who wants to evaluate the truth of a factual claim, uncover new information, or find engaging ideas for personal reflection. Since these kinds of needs present themselves at least occasionally to virtually everyone, library research skills should be part of a person's general education. For our purposes, we are considering research into topics for philosophy papers in higher education. Still, let's begin with the basics.

A library has a catalog, often called the card catalog, that is used to locate books. Periodicals—magazines, journals, and other literature that are issued periodically—are located by using an appropriate periodical index. A working knowledge of these information-locating tools is important. Familiarity with encyclopedias, almanacs, and other special reference sources is also desirable.

The Catalog

Every library has a catalog that records each book in the library's collection and indicates its location on the library shelves. Periodicals are sometimes listed here as well. Many libraries have a traditional "card catalog," with three-by-five-inch cards filed in drawers of one or more filing cabinets. Although a major library may have a dozen or more large cabinets, locating a book is a relatively simple matter. The library's patrons—its customers—have direct access to the catalog, but the library staff should be quite willing to lend a hand if you need help. In some libraries, the catalog is recorded on microfiche (pronounced "microfeesh")—sheets of microfilm—instead of the traditional paper cards. In other libraries, access to catalog information is partially or wholly computerized.

Each book has at least three separate listings in the catalog. It is listed alphabetically by the author's name, by the book's title, and by the general subject of the book. Often, the author and title files are merged, and the subject file is separate. The organization of the catalog, however, varies among libraries.

If you are looking for a specific book, you can use either the author's name or the book's title to discover whether the library has the book in its collection and, if so, where it is located. If you want to find out which books by a specific author are available in this library, you can find them recorded alphabetically under the author's name in the catalog. If you have no specific book in mind, or if you have forgotten both the author's name and the book's title, you can use the subject listings to search the collection.

Searching by subject can be tricky. The subject category you have selected may list so many books that you must spend more time than you desire going through the list. Furthermore, you may be using a wrong subject category for your search. You may, for example, be looking within the category "Insanity," while the best book for your purposes is recorded under "Mentally Ill," a heading you haven't considered. To help with this problem you can consult *Library of Congress Subject Headings*, a two-volume work for standardization of subject categories and for cross-referencing categories, or *Sears List of Subject Headings*, depending on which is used by that library.

Many libraries—public, private, and academic—are part of a library network. These networks enable member libraries to borrow books from the collections of other member libraries for use by their patrons. For practical purposes, this can significantly extend the holdings of a library. Many of these networks maintain a catalog of books that is available on microfiche or by computer at each member library and branch.

In cataloging books, libraries use either the Dewey decimal system or the Library of Congress system, both of which classify books by subject. Each book in the collection has a different *call number*. This code, recorded with each catalog entry, is printed on the spine of the book and dictates the book's location on the shelves.

These are the major categories of the Dewey decimal classification:

000:	GENERALITIES
100:	PHILOSOPHY
200:	RELIGION
300:	SOCIAL SCIENCES
400:	LANGUAGE
500:	PURE SCIENCES
600:	TECHNOLOGY (APPLIED SCIENCES)
700:	FINE ARTS
800:	LITERATURE
900:	GEOGRAPHY AND HISTORY

Each hundred-level category is further divided according to distinctions within that area. For example, the 100 category, which includes philosophy, contains the following classifications:

100:	Philosophy and related disciplines
110:	Metaphysics
120:	Epistemology, causation, humankind
130:	Paranormal phenomena and arts

140:   Specific philosophical viewpoints

150:   Psychology

160:   Logic

170:   Ethics (moral philosophy)

180:   Ancient, medieval, Oriental

190:   Modern Western philosophy

For the Library of Congress classification, these are the major categories:

A: GENERAL WORKS

B: PHILOSOPHY, PSYCHOLOGY, RELIGION

C: AUXILIARY SCIENCES OF HISTORY

D: HISTORY: GENERAL AND OLD WORLD

E–F: HISTORY: AMERICA

G: GEOGRAPHY

H: SOCIAL SCIENCES

J: POLITICAL SCIENCE

K: LAW

L: EDUCATION

M: MUSIC AND BOOKS ON MUSIC

N: FINE ARTS

P: LANGUAGE AND LITERATURE

Q: SCIENCE

R: MEDICINE

S: AGRICULTURE

T: TECHNOLOGY

U: MILITARY SCIENCE

V: NAVAL SCIENCE

Z: BIBLIOGRAPHY, LIBRARY SCIENCE

Each single-letter category is further divided, as with the Dewey decimal system, according to distinctions within that area. For example, the B category, which includes philosophy, contains the following classifications:

B: Philosophy (general)

BC: Logic

BD: Speculative philosophy

BF: Psychology, parapsychology, occult sciences

BH: Aesthetics

BJ: Ethics

BL: Religions, mythology, rationalism

BM: Judaism

BP: Islam, Bahaism, Theosophy, etc.

BQ: Buddhism

BR: Christianity

BS: The Bible

BT: Doctrinal theology

BV: Practical theology

BX: Christian denominations

Now let's examine a card catalog's author card, title card, and subject-heading card for one book: *Philosophy and the Mirror of Nature*, by Richard Rorty, a respected contemporary philosopher. These cards are typical of card-catalog entries, but the microfiche and computer formats may offer less information per entry.

Figure 3 shows the author card for Professor Rorty's book. It is located by finding the correct drawer in the card catalog and searching alphabetically. You might find this card in a drawer labeled ROOS-ROSS.

The call number, B/53/.R68, is in the upper left corner of the card. The first line of print shows the author's name. The last name is printed first because it determines the card's placement in the catalog. Below the author's name is the book's title. On this particular card, the remaining information in that paragraph is a restatement of the author's name, the place of publication, the publishing company, and the date of publication. Below this are listed the number of prefatory pages (15), the number of text pages (401), and the book size. Near the bottom of the card are the subject headings under which the book is listed. For some books, there is only one subject heading. Here there are six. The

Figure 3

```
B
53
. R68        Rorty, Richard.
                Philosophy and the mirror of nature /
             Richard Rorty. -- Princeton : Princeton
             University Press, c1979.
                xv, 401 p. ; 22 cm.
                Includes bibliographical references
             and index.
                ISBN 0-691-07236-1


                1. Philosophy.   2. Philosophy,
             Modern.   3. Mind and body.   4.
             Representation (Philosophy)   5.
             Analysis (Philosophy)   6. Civilization
             --Philosophy.   I. Title


        25 AUG 92       5886457   CPDAsl        79-84013
```

codes along the very bottom of the card are for use by the library's cataloging staff.

Figure 4 shows the title card for Professor Rorty's book. It is located in the same alphabetically ordered catalog as the author's card. Again, the call number is in the upper left corner of the card. The information on this card is the same as that on the author's card. The only difference is that here the title of the book is printed at the top of the card because this is what determines the placement of this card in the catalog.

Figure 5 shows a subject-heading card for Professor Rorty's book. In many libraries, remember, the subject-heading cards will be in a separate catalog file from the author and title cards.

This book was entered in the subject catalog under six subject-headings: (1) Philosophy, (2) Philosophy, Modern, (3) Mind and body, (4) Representation (Philosophy), (5) Analysis (Philosophy), and (6) Civilization—Philosophy. The card illustrated here is the one that files *Philosophy and the Mirror of Nature* under "Analysis (Philosophy)," in one of the *A* drawers. Remember to check *Library of Congress Subject Headings* or *Sears List of Subject Headings* for direction in selecting a subject heading.

Figure 4

```
                    Philosophy and the mirror of nature

B
53
.R68          Rorty, Richard.
                   Philosophy and the mirror of nature /
              Richard Rorty. -- Princeton : Princeton
              University Press, c1979.
                   xv, 401 p. ; 22 cm.
                   Includes bibliographical references
              and index.
                   ISBN 0-691-07236-1


                   1. Philosophy.   2. Philosophy,
              Modern.   3. Mind and body.   4.
              Representation (Philosophy)  5.
              Analysis (Philosophy)  6. Civilization
              --Philosophy.   I. Title


              25 AUG 92      5886457  CPDAnt       79-84013
```

Figure 5

```
                    ANALYSIS (PHILOSOPHY)

B
53
.R68          Rorty, Richard.
                   Philosophy and the mirror of nature /
              Richard Rorty. -- Princeton : Princeton
              University Press, c1979.
                   xv, 401 p. ; 22 cm.
                   Includes bibliographical references
              and index.
                   ISBN 0-691-07236-1


                   1. Philosophy.   2. Philosophy,
              Modern.   3. Mind and body.   4.
              Representation (Philosophy)  5.
              Analysis (Philosophy)  6. Civilization
              --Philosophy.   I. Title


              25 AUG 92      5886457  CPDAsc        79-84013
```

Periodical Indexes

Periodicals are sometimes included in the library's main catalog. If not, you can discover which periodicals the library subscribes to by consulting its serials list, an alphabetical compilation of the names of all the library's periodicals. The way in which periodicals are filed varies among libraries. The current issue is usually available for patrons to read while they are in the library building. Previous issues ("back issues") may be in "closed stacks." This means that the shelves are not open to the patrons. If this is the case, the library staff retrieves the desired issue. If the library has "open stacks" for periodicals, the patron may go directly to the shelves that hold the previous issues. Periodicals may be ordered alphabetically or by call number on these shelves. Some libraries allow patrons to sign periodicals out of the library, but many do not.

Imagine that you are writing a paper for which you need to find a certain kind of article, or even a specific article, from a periodical. You can quickly and easily search through years of issues for dozens, or even hundreds, of periodicals by using a periodical index.

You should know the major periodical indexes and be able to use them. The following paragraphs describe the basics of the *Readers' Guide*, the *Magazine Index*, and the *National Newspaper Index*.

The Readers' Guide to Periodical Literature, better known simply as the *Readers' Guide*, indexes articles from more than 160 periodicals. These periodicals are identified at the beginning of each of the volumes in the set. Published by the W. H. Wilson Company and with indexing back to 1890, these volumes list articles that you can use in constructing or evaluating argumentation. Fiction, reviews, and poetry are also indexed. However, the magazines indexed here are general readership magazines rather than specialized periodicals for professionals in a certain field. You must exercise good judgment in using these sources because the *Readers' Guide* does not screen articles for quality. In assessing the reliability of the material, you have to consider the character and readership of the publication and available information about the author.

New articles are indexed and the index is published monthly for six months of the year and twice a month for six months.

Each year, the material from the previous calendar year's monthly and semimonthly paperback issues is published in a single hardcover "cumulative" volume. The new volume then becomes a part of the permanent set of *Readers' Guide* volumes. (Before 1985, volumes were not based on the calendar year.)

Under subject and author categories, articles are listed alphabetically by title. Cross-referencing to related categories is provided where appropriate, so you won't have to guess about subject categories. Figure 6 shows a sample entry. This entry on civil rights can be found on pages 37 and 38 of the (temporary)

Figure 6

CIVIL RIGHTS
 See also
 Authors' rights
 Citizenship
 Civil Rights Act of 1991
 Freedom of speech
 Freedom of the press
 Homeless—Civil rights
 Right of privacy
 Right of property
 Searches and seizures
 Women—Equal rights

Activists face increased harassment. C. Berlet. il *Utne Reader* p85-8 Ja/F '92
International aspects
Human rights: an international responsibility [address, February 10, 1992] D. Quayle. *US Department of State Dispatch* 3:103-4 F 17 '92
China
The Beijing-Tokyo axis against human rights. Liu Binyan. *New Perspectives Quarterly* 9:31-3 Wint '92
The East Asian way [interview with Lee Kuan Yew] N. Gardels. *New Perspectives Quarterly* 9:4-9+ Wint '92
No double standard for Asia. Fang Lizhi. il *New Perspectives Quarterly* 9:30-1 Wint '92
U.S. human rights policy is garbage [views of Chinese officials] D. Schlesinger. *New Perspectives Quarterly* 9:33 Wint '92
Haiti
'Backers' [forced repatriation of Haitian refugees] A. Husarska. *The New Republic* 206:16+ Mr 16 '92
South Africa
 See also
 Apartheid
United States
 See Civil rights

paperback supplement for the period of March 6–19, 1992. The articles listed here will become part of the permanent volume 92 of *Readers' Guide*. The *see* or *see also* referencing cue indicates that related articles are listed under the other subject categories named there. After a listing for "Activists face increased harassment" by C. Berlet in the *Utne Reader*, other articles are listed under the subheadings "International aspects," "China," and "Haiti." Reference cues are given for the subheadings "South Africa" and "United States."

In alphabetizing the articles, *a*, *an*, and *the* are disregarded. In the sample entry, then, the first two articles under the subheading "China" begin with *The*, while the third one begins with *No*. Let's take that third article as a sample entry. The title, "No double standard for Asia," is followed by the author's name, Fang Lizhi. The *il* indicates that the article is illustrated. It can be found in *New Perspectives Quarterly*, volume 9, pages 30 through 31. It is in the Winter 1992 issue. All entries can be read in this way. In some cases (four, in this civil rights category), square brackets, which the publisher calls "title enhancement," are added to clarify the topic of the article. General instructions for using the *Readers' Guide* and a key to abbreviations are printed in the first few pages of each volume.

Figure 7 shows a sample entry for which the category is a person's name. This is the entry for the British philosopher Bertrand Russell in volume 5 (1919–1921). Articles Professor Russell wrote are listed before articles about him. This is the standard procedure in the *Readers' Guide*. A portrait is included where *por* is indicated.

Besides the general *Readers' Guide*, W. H. Wilson Company publishes many specialized indexes: *Applied Science and Technology Index, Art Index, Biography Index, Biological and Agricultural Index, Business Periodicals Index, Education Index, General Science Index, Humanities Index* (including philosophical topics), *Index to Legal Periodicals, Social Science Index*, and others. For these publications, indexing is the same as in the *Readers' Guide*. Other publishers produce useful periodical indexes too. One puts out an annual *Consumers Index to Product Evaluations and Information Sources*. Another produces *Access*, a recent index to supplement other general indexes. Many magazines publish indexes to their

Figure 7

> **Russell, Bertrand Arthur William**
> Bolshevik theory. New Repub 24:67-9, 239-41,
> 296-8 S 15, N 3, 17 '20
> Democracy and direct action.   Dial 66:445-8
> My 3 '19
> Dreams and facts. Dial 68:214-20 F '20
> Economic unity and political division.   Dial
> 66:629-31 Je 28 '19
> Impressions of bolshevist Russia. Liv Age
> 306:387-91 Ag 14 '20
> Industry in undeveloped countries. Atlan 127:
> 787-95 Je '21
> Socialism and liberal ideals. Liv Age 306:114-
> 23 Jl 10 '20
> Soviet Russia—1920. Nation 111:121-6, 152-4
> Jl 31-Ag 7 '20
> Why and wherefore of wishing for things.
> Liv Age 304:528-33 F 28 '20
> Bertrand Russell on Russia. New Repub 24:
> 6-7 S 1 '20
> Bertrand Russell on socialism. G. A. Kleene.
> Q J Econ 34:756-62 Ag '20
> Bertrand Russell prophecies the speedy tri-
> umph of socialism. por Cur   Opinion 68:
> 813-15 Je '20
> Rex vs. Bertrand Russell. Liv Age 300:385-94
> F 15 '19
> Thought of Bertrand Russell. Liv Age 310:
> 585-9 S 3 '21
> Three philosopher-prophets. A. McDowall.
> Liv Age 310:200-8 Jl 23 '21

own back issues. *National Geographic, Scientific American,* and *The Saturday Review* are among these.

The *Magazine Index,* available at an increasing number of libraries, has an advantage over the *Readers' Guide:* It indexes more than four hundred periodicals, doubling the resources of the *Readers' Guide.* A disadvantage, however, is that it indexes articles in those periodicals for only the previous four years. (Microfiche records of the *Magazine Index* entries dating back to 1977 are available.) Each index, then, provides something the other doesn't. When you want a wide range of sources and you are interested in recent articles, you should use the *Magazine Index.* On the other hand, when you need to research articles that are not recent, such as popular articles written by Bertrand Russell, the *Readers' Guide* is the reference tool to use.

The *Magazine Index* is not bound in volumes that await you on a shelf. It is available on microfilm or computer. In the microfilm format, the information is displayed on the screen of an $18 \times 18 \times 15$-inch desktop machine. When you switch the machine on, you view an illuminated microfilm. You can locate the desired section of film by using the simple controls on the right side of the machine. The same index is available by computer, and it can be accessed on-line, with CD-ROM, or by computer tape.

In the single index, you can find subject categories, author categories, product (brand name) categories, and entries for reviews of movies, restaurants, books, and plays. The reviews are graded (A, B, C, D, F) to indicate the reviewer's general evaluation.

Unlike the *Readers' Guide*, the listings within a category are not alphabetical but are according to date, with the most recent articles listed first. If the same word refers to a subject or title and to people (for example, "Carpenter"), the people are entered last. Finally, not all authors are listed. A person is listed as author only if that person is also the subject of an article that is listed in the *Magazine Index* or if a review of that person's work is listed in the index.

The *National Newspaper Index* is similar in format to the *Magazine Index*; both are products of Information Access Company, a division of Ziff-Davis Publishing Company. This index lists articles from *Wall Street Journal*, *New York Times*, *Christian Science Monitor*, *Los Angeles Times*, and *Washington Post*. Again, recent articles are listed first. Many libraries also have back issues of certain newspapers and periodicals available on rolls of microfilm that can be read on a microfilm-reader machine. There is a microfilm version of *The New York Times* for issues as early as 1851 and of the London *Times* for issues as early as 1785.

Other General Resources

Sometimes the best source of information for your needs is one of those books or sets of books that has been designed specifically for reference use. Hundreds, or even thousands, of useful publications of this kind await discovery in a full-service library.

The names of several prominent encyclopedias, almanacs, atlases, gazetteers, and other reference sources are mentioned in this section.

Encyclopedias

Although some single-volume or two-volume works are also termed "encyclopedias," the word typically refers to a set of twenty to thirty volumes. The presentation in a general encyclopedia is intended as introductory; specialized encyclopedias such as *The Encyclopedia of Philosophy* are exceptions. Topics included range from geographic locations ("Paris," "Africa," "Greece") to people ("Bertrand Russell," "Aristotle," "Nelson Mandela") to events ("World War II," "Renaissance," "Reformation") to general topics ("tariff," "violence," "vegetarianism").

The New Encyclopaedia Britannica is the most scholarly and generally the most detailed encyclopedia. The new format of the *Britannica* is designed to offer in-depth coverage without being cumbersome for the person who wants a quick and less-detailed presentation. Essentially, it is two complete encyclopedia sets: the *Micropaedia* for "Ready Reference" and the *Macropaedia* for "Knowledge in Depth." A companion volume, the *Propaedia*, offered as an "Outline of Knowledge," presents an extensive overview of the branches of human inquiry. Since 1986, there has also been a two-volume index. The *Britannica* has especially thorough presentations of scientific topics.

Other major encyclopedias are *Academic American, Collier's, Encyclopedia Americana*, and *World Book. Academic American* was the first encyclopedia available on-line, and *Encyclopedia Americana* emphasizes American life and institutions.

Almanacs, Atlases, And Gazetteers

An **almanac** is an annual compilation of detailed statistical, historical, geographic, educational, athletic, and miscellaneous information. The favorite almanacs today are *Information Please Almanac, World Almanac*, and *Reader's Digest Almanac and Yearbook*.

Thematic almanacs focus on specific areas of interest. Examples of thematic almanacs are *Catholic Almanac, The*

Statesman's Year-Book (from Great Britain), and the two-volume *Europa Yearbook*, which contains details on all the nations of the world.

An **atlas** is a book of maps. The London *Times* sponsors the preparation of an excellent international atlas, *The Times Atlas of the World*. In the United States, major atlases are published by Rand McNally, Hammond, and *Reader's Digest*. Hammond's *Medallion World Atlas* includes an historical atlas section and maps of the Bible lands. The National Geographic Society and *Goode's* also publish good atlases. Thematic atlases are available as well.

A **gazetteer** is a dictionary of geographical information, defining names like Bosnia, Azerbaijan, Baghdad, Troy, Suez Canal, Mount Whitney, and Amazon. Correct pronunciation is also indicated. *Webster's New Geographical Dictionary* and the *International Geographical Encyclopedia and Atlas* are among the respected gazetteers. Of course, the breakup of the Soviet Union and the continual sovereignty shifts in Eastern Europe have caused quite a scramble in the atlas and gazetteer business. You cannot idly assume that your geographical research sources are up-to-date.

Special Reference Sources

Even a general survey of additional reference sources would be extensive. Instead, a few specific sources are mentioned. For a better sense of the range of special reference volumes, visit a good library.

Books in Print lists the title, author or editor, publisher, and price of almost every book that is published or exclusively distributed in the United States and is currently in print. Three volumes are indexed by author, three by title, and several by subject. In addition, special volumes augment/append the basic set: a two-volume midyear supplement and some volumes on paperbound books in print. A new set of *Books in Print* is published each year. There is even a set called *Forthcoming Books*. The *Cumulative Book Index*, another publication, is the massive result of an attempt to list all books that have been printed in English, whether they are in or out of print. Each year, a volume listing new books is added to the set.

Facts on File is "a weekly news digest of world events with a thorough, cumulative index." Its issues are filed in large ring binders and they date back to 1940.

Many useful directories can be found in a library. For example, information on colleges and universities can be found in *The College Blue Book* (5 volumes), *Lovejoy's College Guide*, and *The Gourman Report: A Rating of Undergraduate Programs in American and International Universities*. Other examples of directories are *The Official Museum Directory* and the three-volume *Directory of Associations*. There is even a *Directory of Directories!*

The United States government publishes many informative booklets and handbooks. For example, the Bureau of the Census produces the *Statistical Abstract of the United States*, an impressive collection of statistical data from private and public sources, focusing on the social, political, and economic structure of the nation. *The U. S. Government Manual* lists government agencies and addresses. For an extensive list of government publications, many of which are free, you can write to the U. S. Government Printing Office, Washington, D. C. 20402.

Resources in Philosophy

Philosophy papers do not always display special philosophical terminology (e.g., "epistemology" or "transcendental"). They do not always focus on technical or academic issues, or on historical philosophers or movements. Many papers in ethics, for example, address social issues in a nontechnical but still thought-provoking way, using compelling argumentation to establish a point about rights, obligations, or justice. Such a paper may be written without the use of any specifically philosophical books or articles.

At other times, a philosophy paper calls for the use of resources with a specific philosophical focus. Reference books in philosophy may be used, or a search for journal articles may be needed. Here you will find an introduction to resources in philosophy.

Special Volumes in Philosophy

The Encyclopedia of Philosophy, edited by Paul Edwards and published by Macmillan Publishing Company and The Free Press, may be the best known of the special reference books in philosophy. It was originally published in eight volumes. Now it is *bound* as four books, with the original volumes one and two bound together, the original volumes three and four bound together, and so on. The new version still has the original title pages (the title page for volume two now occurs mid-book) and pagination begins again with each of the eight original volumes. When referencing this source, consider it as an eight-volume work.

The Encyclopedia of Philosophy has articles on philosophers, philosophical movements, and philosophical concepts, as well as articles on topics that are related to philosophy though less directly. Here are some examples:

Philosophers	*Philosophical Movements*
Berkeley, George	Empiricism
Camus, Albert	Enlightenment
Frege, Gottlob	Hegelianism
Marcel, Gabriel	Idealism
Maritain, Jacques	Marxist philosophy
Nicholas of Cusa	Phenomenology
Ortega y Gasset, José	Polish philosophy
Pascal, Blaise	Rationalism
Peirce, Charles Sanders	Pragmatism
Schopenhauer, Arthur	Skepticism

Philosophical Concepts	*Related Articles*
Causation	Asceticism
Consciousness	Darwinism
Definition	Emotion and Feeling
God, concepts of	Illusions
Induction	Life, origin of
Knowledge and belief	Myth
Responsibility	Organismic Biology
Sensa	Psychology
Substance and attribute	Racism
Teleology	Religion and science

The articles in *The Encyclopedia of Philosophy* are more easily understood by advanced undergraduates and graduate students in philosophy. Terms like epistemological may be used, for example, without explanation. Still, beginners in academic philosophy frequently benefit significantly from these rather thorough overviews written by respected contemporary philosophers.

Other reference works in which philosophical topics are explained are the *Dictionary of Philosophy*, by Dagobert D. Runes, *Greek Philosophical Terms: A Historical Lexicon*, by F. E. Peters, and *The Concise Encyclopedia of Western Philosophy and Philosophers*, which is edited by James O. Urmson.

Histories of philosophy that take up one or more volumes are also available. Among these are Will Durant's classic *The Story of Philosophy*, Frederick Copleston's detailed and respected *A History of Philosophy*, Wallace I. Matson's well-written *A New History of Philosophy*, John Herman Randall, Jr.'s *The Career of Philosophy*, W. T. Jones's old standard *A History of Western Philosophy*, and Bertrand Russell's entertaining and occasionally idiosyncratic work of the same title, *A History of Western Philosophy*. Of these, only Durant's and Russell's books are in a single volume. Each of these histories of philosophy, however, is available in paperback. In addition, several shorter "outlines" of the history of philosophy have been published.

For some philosophers, there are books that are bibliographies of their own written work and/or the "literature" on them—articles and books about that philosopher's views. The Philosophy Documentation Center at Bowling Green State University, directed by Richard H. Lineback, publishes some of these bibliographies. So far, the center has published bibliographies on Bergson, Bradley, Heidegger, Hobbes, Husserl, Ortega y Gasset, Paul of Venice, Peirce, Santayana, Sartre, Vico (works in English only), and Whitehead.

Philosophy Books, 1982–1986, published by the center, is a bibliography with abstracts of the 650 philosophy books written in English and published during 1982–1986 and most often referred to in other published work during 1987–1989.

The Philosophy Documentation Center also publishes the *International Directory of Philosophy* and the *Directory of American Philosophers*, with information on philosophy programs in colleges and universities, philosophical institutes and societies, journals, and publishers.

Philosophical Journals

Scholarly academic journals in particular academic disciplines are periodicals to which scholars and libraries subscribe. In philosophy journals, most articles are written by professors. Occasionally, however, a published article is written by a scholar who is not affiliated with the faculty of an educational institution.

Besides articles (ranging in length from a few pages to thirty or forty pages), philosophical journals may publish less formal "discussions," responses to other articles, and reviews of new books in the field.

Because journal discourse is typically intended for other scholars in the field, it is sometimes difficult for students to read. Technical language is often employed, and familiarity with previous work on the topic (in articles or books) may be assumed. The accessibility to undergraduates varies among journals and articles. Sometimes no preparation at all is assumed.

The contents of an issue, with each article's title and author, are listed on the front cover, on the back cover, or on one of the opening pages. The institutional affiliation of the author is often indicated at the beginning or end of each article. Here is a partial list of well-known journals in philosophy that publish most articles in English:

American Philosophical Quarterly

Analysis

Ancient Philosophy

The Australasian Journal of Philosophy

Dialectica

Dialogue

Ethics

Inquiry

International Philosophical Quarterly

Journal of Aesthetics and Art Criticism

Journal of Philosophy

Journal of Value Inquiry

Mind

Monist

Nous

Philosophical Quarterly
Philosophical Review
Philosophy
Philosophy and Phenomenological Research
Philosophy and Public Affairs
Philosophy East and West
Ratio
Review of Metaphysics
Theoria
Thought

The Philosopher's Index

The Philosopher's Index catalogs philosophy books, anthologies, and individual articles from journals and anthologies. It is published quarterly in paperback and a hardcover cumulative edition is published annually. This publication of the Philosophy Documentation Center indexes philosophical work from more than forty countries, although most of it is from North America and Western Europe.

Works are indexed by subject and author. As an sample of the subject index, examine page 19 of the 1968 cumulative edition of *The Philosopher's Index*, which is shown in Figure 8. As a sample of the author index, examine page 655 of the same volume, which is shown in Figure 9.

Through the annual editions of *The Philosopher's Index* and a special retrospective index, you can find bibliographic references to thousands of books and journal articles published since 1940.

On-line computer access to *The Philosopher's Index* provides searches by subject, year, author, or journal via DIALOG or KNOWLEDGE INDEX. Also available are a tutorial manual titled *Searching the Philosopher's Index Database*, a subject heading index titled *The Philosopher's Index Thesaurus*, and a CD-ROM version of *The Philosopher's Index*. For a catalog describing the offerings of the Philosophy Documentation Center, you can call (419) 372-2419 or (800) 444-2419, or you can write to the center's staff at Bowling Green State University, Bowling Green, Ohio 43403–0189.

Figure 8

SUBJECT INDEX 19

AMERICAN	A NOTE ON HENRY WINTHROPS AMERICAN NATIONAL CHARACTER AND THE EXISTENTIALIST POSTURE. CYRIL WELCH. J EXISTENT 7,243-249 WINT 66-67
AMERICAN	AMBIVALENCE IN AMERICAN POLITICAL PHILOSOPHY. FRED KRINSKY. PERSONALIST 48,89-102 JA 67
AMERICAN	BEAUTIFICATION RECONSIDERED. THOMAS MUNRO. J AES EDUC 1,85-100 SPR 66
AMERICAN	L A CREMINS APPRECIATION OF AMERICAN EDUCATION. WILLIAM W BRICKMAN. J THOUGHT 3,80-89 AP 68
AMERICAN	PHILOSOPHY OF EDUCATION IN THE UNITED STATES. HARRY S BROUDY. PROC PHIL EDUC 22,1-10 1966
AMERICAN	RUSSIAN AND THE U S A, A CHALLENGE TO THE CONVERGENCE THEORY. BERTRAM D WOLFE. HUMANIST 28,3-8 S-O 68
AMERICAN	THE FRONTIER THESIS AND THE DEPRESSION. STEVEN KESSELMAN. J HIST IDEAS 29,253-268 AP-JE 68
AMERICAN	THE INDIAN INFLUENCE IN AMERICAN PHILOSOPHY, EMERSON TO MOORE. DALE RIEPE. PHIL EAST WEST 17,125-137 JA-O 67
AMERICAN	THE INFLUENCE OF MARXS THOUGHT IN THE UNITED STATES. HOWARD L PARSONS. PRAXIS 3,264-275 1967
AMERICAN	THE NEGATIVISM OF POLITICAL GOALS. WAYNE A R LEYS. ANTIOCH REV 28,215-224 SUM 68
AMERICAN	THE PHILOSOPHICAL BACKGROUND TO THE FABLE OF EMERSONS AMERICAN SCHOLAR. SACVAN BERCOVITCH. J HIST IDEAS 28,123-128 JA-MR 67
AMERICAN	WHAT ARE THE PRINCIPLES OF AMERICAN CONSTITUTIONAL LAW. ROBERT GOEDECKE. ETHICS 78,17-31 O 67
AMES,W	TECHNOMETRIA, PURITAN THEOLOGY. KEITH L SPRUNGER. J HIST IDEAS 29,115-122 JA-MR 68
AMIEL,H	AMIELS NEW PHENOMENOLOGY. HERBERT SPIEGELBERG. ARCH GESCH PHIL 49,201-214 1967
ANALOGY	AESTHETICS OF ANALOGY. ERIC LAGUARDIA. DIOGENES 62,49-61 SUMMER 68
ANALOGY	ANALOGY IN QUANTUM THEORY, FROM INSIGHT TO NONSENSE. MARIO BUNGE. BRIT J PHIL SCI 18,265-286 F 68
ANALOGY	HYPOTHESIS, ANALOGY, AND TYPIFICATION AS METHODOLOGICAL TECHNIQUES FOR SOCIETAL KNOWLEDGE. D I CHESNOKOV. SOVIET STUD PHIL 5,21-32 WINT 66-67
ANALOGY	UNIVOCALISM IN CAJETANS DOCTRINE OF ANALOGY. MICHAEL MCCANLES. NEW SCHOLAS 42,18-47 WINT 68
ANALYSIS	A NEW LOOK AT LINGUISTIC ANALYSIS. JOHN KOZY, JR. S J PHIL 5,155-159 FALL 67
ANALYSIS	ANALYSIS AND THE PHILOSOPHY OF SCIENCE. EDWARD MACKINNON. INT PHIL QUART 7,213-250 JE 67
ANALYSIS	CONTEMPORARY PHILOSOPHY AND THE ANALYTIC-SYNTHETIC DICHOTOMY. STUART C HACKETT. INT PHIL QUART 7,413-440 S 67

Figure 9

AUTHOR INDEX 655

RADER, MELVIN. MARXS INTERPRETATION OF ART AND AESTHETIC VALUE. BRIT J AES 7,237-249 JL 67

RADFORD, COLIN. KNOWING BUT NOT BELIEVING. ANALYSIS 27,139-140 MR 67

RADNER, MICHAEL AND BUB, JEFFREY. MILLERS PARADOX OF INFORMATION. BRIT J PHIL SCI 19,63-67 MY 68

RAFIQUE, M. SRI AUROBINDOS CRITIQUE OF MATERIALISM AND IDEALISM. DARSHANA INT 7,10-14 O 67

RAINE, KATHLEEN. THOMAS TAYLOR, PLATO AND THE ENGLISH ROMANTIC MOVEMENT. BRIT J AES 8,99-123 AP 68

RAJAN, R SANDARA. CASSIRER AND WITTGENSTEIN. INT PHIL QUART 7,591-610 67

RAJAN, R SUNDARA. WITTGENSTEINS CONCEPTION OF CRITERION. J INDIAN ACAD PHIL 6,45-58 1967

RALEIGH, HENRY P. THE PROBLEM OF EXPRESSION IN ART AND ART EDUCATION. J AES 2,85-95 AP 68

RAM, ALUR JANAKI. ARJUNA AND HAMLET, TWO MORAL DILEMMAS. PHIL EAST WEST 18,11-28 JA-AP 68

RAMA RAO, P S S. THE THEISTIC HUMANISM OF PAUL A SCHILPP. DARSHANA INT 6,52-61 O 66

RAMNOUX, C. ETUDES PRESOCRATIQUES,III, HIPPOLYTE, CONTRE LES HERESIES, VII,383 A 399 I. REV PHIL FR 157,31-41 JA-MR 67

RANDALL, JOHN HERMAN, JR. F H BRADLEY AND THE WORKING-OUT OF ABSOLUTE IDEALISM. J HIST PHIL 5,245-267 JL 67

RANDALL, JOHN HERMAN, JR. METAPHYSICS AND LANGUAGE. REV METAPH 20,591-601 JE 67

RANDALL, JOHN HERMAN, JR. PLATOS TREATMENT OF THE THEME OF THE GOOD LIFE AND HIS CRITICISM OF THE SPARTAN IDEAL. J HIST IDEAS 28,307-324 JL-S 67

RANKEN, NANI L. A NOTE ON DUCASSES PERCEIVABLE CAUSATION. PHIL PHENOMENOL RES 28,269-270 D 67

RANKEN, NANI L. A NOTE ON PAST AND FUTURE FUTURES. PHIL PHENOMENOL RES 27,615-617 JE 67

RANKEN, NANI L. THE UNMOVED AGENT AND THE GROUND OF RESPONSIBILITY. J PHIL 64,403-408 JL 6 67

RANKIN, H D. GILBERT RYLES PLATOS PROGRESS. AUSTL J PHIL 45,104-113 MY 67

RANKIN, K W. EXISTENCE AND TIME. PHIL PHENOMENOL RES 27,199-215 D 66

RANKIN, K W. PAST AND FUTURE. PHIL QUART 17,317-333 O 67

RANKIN, K W. THE ROLE OF IMAGINATION, RULE-OPERATIONS, AND ATMOSPHERE IN WITTGENSTEINS LANGUAGE-GAMES. INQUIRY 10,279-291 FALL 67

RANKIN, NANI L. METAPHYSICAL FREEDOM AND THE DETERMINATION OF RESPONSIBILITY. J VALUE INQ 1,184-189 WINT 67-68

RANTA, JERRALD. THE DRAMA OF PLATOS ION. J AES ART CRIT 26,219-229 WINT 67

Appendix

A Sample Paper in Two Documentation Formats

The following sample paper on the pre-Socratic philosophers from Miletus is shown first with endnote documentation. For footnote documentation, the only difference is that each note would appear at the bottom of the page on which the reference is indicated. No bibliography or "Works Cited" section is included. Remember that item is sometimes omitted if you use note documentation.

The same paper is then shown with parenthetical documentation. Parenthetical references, usually indicating only author and page reference, direct the reader to the appropriate bibliographic entry in the Works Cited list.

The first version of the sample paper with endnote documentation starts on the following page. The second version with parenthetical documentation starts on page 119.

The Milesians:

Three Giant Steps Forward

Diane Shipley

Knowledge and Reality

Philosophy 101

Palomar College

March 6, 1992

This version of the sample paper uses endnote documentation.

1

The philosophers of ancient Miletus held views about
nature that sound simple-minded to us today. Thales
said that we can comprehend nature by understanding
that water is the source of all things. Anaximander said
that everything started in a flux called apeiron.
Anaximenes said that everything is a form of air. The
views sound primitive. The thinkers sound naive. But,
though one view seems hardly an improvement on the
previous one, that is not really so. I claim that each of
the Milesian philosophers, in turn, makes important
observations and displays a significant advance in thinking over the preceding one. I will begin by showing that
Thales' view was a result of reflection rather than an
arbitrary selection of water as the basic stuff of the
universe. Then I will show that there is significant advance in Anaximander's move to a nonphysical principle
and Anaximenes' quantitative analysis of matter.

Thales

Thales, who flourished around 585 B.C., when he is said
to have predicted a solar eclipse,[1] believed either that

2

everything was water or that water was the source of all things.[2] This we understand from fragments of his writings, which is all we have of his work, or, for that matter, of the other Milesians. It may sound silly to us to hear the claim that all is water, but we must put ourselves in the historical context of Thales. He found moisture in all living things, and the water of the high seas seemed hylozoistic (self-moving) just like living beings.[3] In his seaside culture, it may have seemed that everything in life from trade to crops depended on the neighboring Mediterranean Sea. Of the four substances then thought to be basic in the world--earth, air, fire, and water--Thales' choice resulted from observation and reflection. He didn't have the perspective of modern science to make this view sound foolish.

When earlier peoples explained natural events in terms of the emotions and will of deities, great and minor,[4] Thales and the Milesians looked for a natural explanation for change and variety. When they looked around them, they saw change, and it seemed to need explanation. Why was there change? It could be

3

explained in terms of some principle of permanence.
Why was there diversity? It could be explained in terms
of some principle of unity? They tried to explain nature
as an unchanging whole that could be understood without
reference to something outside it, like a god.[5] Nature
was seen as a coherent whole with patterned ways of its
own. By accounting for the change and variety of the
world by reference to one thing to serve as a principle of
unity and permanence, Thales began the history of science. And what better candidate was there than water,
which was present in all living things and perhaps in
everything that exists? How many of us would have
broken out of the superstitions to give a rational--yes,
rational, though not correct--answer?

Anaximander

Anaximander was a later contemporary of Thales,[6] and
he reasoned that no one substance such as water could
ever have been completely dominant. Warring "opposites" such as hot and cold or wet and dry could not

4

have come into being if one of them had ever had exclusive rule over the universe.[7] Instead of naming one substance as basic, Anaximander said that originally everything was in a whirlwind of apeiron. Apeiron means limitless or boundless.[8] This probably meant there was no external limit and no internal distinction between the simple substances of the world.[9] They existed together in one whirling mass, until separate pieces of matter were separated off from the whirl.[10]

Anaximander, then, did not name one substance as basic and primordial. He named a process. By naming an abstract principle, the principle of the boundless, as more basic than any individual substance, he made a scientific advance. He named something that could not be seen and touched in his world. Abstract principles, of course, become basic to modern science. Anaximander made a scientific advance over Thales in the move to an abstract principle for an explanation of the beginnings of the world. And still it was a natural explanation, without divine agents of change.

5

Anaximenes

The last of the three famous Milesian philosophers was Anaximenes.[11] He named air (<u>aer</u> included mists and gases) as the most basic element in the universe. Anaximenes claimed that all substances in our world are the result of either the condensation or the rarefaction of that one elemental substance. Air is constantly moving. Condense it and you get wind, then clouds, water, earth, stones, and all remaining substances. Rarefy air, and you get fire.[12]

It may seem at first as if Anaximenes regressed scientifically from Anaximander's conceiving of an abstract principle to Thales' naming of a single substance. However, Anaximenes no longer was addressing just cosmic beginnings. He was explaining day-to-day natural transformation of substances.[13] And he did introduce another scientific principle. The concept of explaining qualitative differences in quantitative terms is a foundational one in modern science. The differences between substances can be explained by the density of some basic stuff of which the world is made.

6

****

The ancient Milesian philosophers were not, after all,
simple-minded thinkers. Thales' views, based on observation and reflection, were a major advancement over
earlier superstitious, nonnatural accounts of the world.
Anaximander and Anaximenes introduced advances that
are now basic to science: explanation through a principle
of abstraction and quantitative explanation of qualitative
difference. The strides of the Milesians were great. We
would not have modern science without these ideas, and
few of us could have broken through the molds of the
mind to make such breakthroughs if we were in their
position.

7

Notes

[1]Merrill Ring, Beginning with the Pre-Socratics (Mountain View, CA: Mayfield, 1987) 19.

[2]See Ring, 20-21; and G. E. R. Lloyd, Early Greek Science: Thales to Aristotle (New York: Norton, 1970) 18-20. Ring and others believe that Thales characterized all matter as forms of water. Lloyd and others believe that Thales characterized only the origin of the universe when he claimed water as basic.

[3]W. K. C. Guthrie, A History of Greek Philosophy, Vol. 1 (Cambridge: Cambridge University Press, 1962) 62-67.

[4]F. M. Cornford, From Religion to Philosophy (New York: Harper, 1957) 40-72.

[5]Reginald E. Allen, Greek Philosophy: Thales to Aristotle (New York: Free Press, 1966) 2.

[6]Ring, 22.

[7]Lloyd, 20.

[8]F. E. Peters, Greek Philosophical Terms: A Historical Lexicon (New York: New York University Press, 1967) 19-20.

8

[9]W. K. C. Guthrie, <u>The Greek Philosophers: From Thales to Aristotle</u> (New York: Harper, 1950) 27.

[10]———, <u>The Greek Philosophers,</u> 27-28.

[11]Ring, 29.

[12]P. Diamandopoulos, "Anaximenes," <u>Encyclopedia of Philosophy,</u> 1967 ed.

[13]Lloyd, 22.

This version of the sample paper uses parenthetical documentation.

1

The philosophers of ancient Miletus held views about
nature that sound simple-minded to us today. Thales
said that we can comprehend nature by understanding
that water is the source of all things. Anaximander said
that everything started in a flux called <u>apeiron.</u>
Anaximenes said that everything is a form of air. The
views sound primitive. The thinkers sound naive. But,
though one view seems hardly an improvement on the
previous one, that is not really so. I claim that each of
the Milesian philosophers, in turn, makes important
observations and displays a significant advance in thinking over the preceding one. I will begin by showing that
Thales' view was a result of reflection rather than an
arbitrary selection of water as the basic stuff of the
universe. Then I will show that there is significant advance in Anaximander's move to a nonphysical principle
and Anaximenes' quantitative analysis of matter.

<u>Thales</u>

Thales, who flourished around 585 B.C., when he is said
to have predicted a solar eclipse (Ring 19) believed

2

either that everything was water or that water was the
source of all things.[1] This we understand from fragments of his writings, which is all we have of his work,
or, for that matter, of the other Milesians. It may sound
silly to us to hear the claim that all is water, but we
must put ourselves in the historical context of Thales.
He found moisture in all living things, and the water of
the high seas seemed hylozoistic (self-moving) just like
living beings (Guthrie, History 62-67). In his seaside
culture, it may have seemed that everything in life from
trade to crops depended on the neighboring Mediterranean Sea. Of the four substances then thought to be
basic in the world--earth, air, fire, and water--Thales'
choice resulted from observation and reflection. He
didn't have the perspective of modern science to make
this view sound foolish.

  When earlier peoples explained natural events in
terms of the emotions and will of deities, great and minor (Cornford 40-72), Thales and the Milesians looked
for a natural explanation for change and variety. When
they looked around them, they saw change, and it

3

seemed to need explanation. Why was there change? It could be explained in terms of some principle of permanence. Why was there diversity? It could be explained in terms of some principle of unity? They tried to explain nature as an unchanging whole that could be understood without reference to something outside it, like a god (Allen 2). Nature was seen as a coherent whole with patterned ways of its own. By accounting for the change and variety of the world by reference to one thing to serve as a principle of unity and permanence, Thales began the history of science. And what better candidate was there than water, which was present in all living things and perhaps in everything that exists? How many of us would have broken out of the superstitions to give a rational--yes, rational, though not correct--answer?

Anaximander

Anaximander was a later contemporary of Thales (Ring 22), and he reasoned that no one substance such as water could ever have been completely dominant. Warring "opposites" such as hot and cold or wet and dry could not have come into being if one of them had ever

4

had exclusive rule over the universe (Lloyd 20). Instead of naming one substance as basic, Anaximander said that originally everything was in a whirlwind of apeiron. Apeiron means limitless or boundless (Peters 19-20). This probably meant there was no external limit and no internal distinction between the simple substances of the world (Guthrie, Philosophers 27). They existed together in one whirling mass, until separate pieces of matter were separated off from the whirl (Guthrie, Philosophers 27-28).

Anaximander, then, did not name one substance as basic and primordial. He named a process. By naming an abstract principle, the principle of the boundless, as more basic than any individual substance, he made a scientific advance. He named something that could not be seen and touched in his world. Abstract principles, of course, become basic to modern science. Anaximander made a scientific advance over Thales in the move to an abstract principle for an explanation of the beginnings of the world. And still it was a natural explanation, without divine agents of change.

5

Anaximenes

The last of the three famous Milesian philosophers was
Anaximenes (Ring 29). He named air (aer included
mists and gases) as the most basic element in the universe. Anaximenes claimed that all substances in our
world are the result of either the condensation or the
rarefaction of that one elemental substance. Air is constantly moving. Condense it and you get wind, then
clouds, water, earth, stones, and all remaining substances. Rarefy air, and you get fire (Diamandopoulos).

It may seem at first as if Anaximenes regressed scientifically from Anaximander's conceiving of an abstract
principle to Thales' naming of a single substance. However, Anaximenes no longer was addressing just cosmic
beginnings. He was explaining day-to-day natural transformation of substances (Lloyd 22). And he did introduce another scientific principle. The concept of explaining qualitative differences in quantitative terms is a
foundational one in modern science. The differences
between substances can be explained by the density of
some basic stuff of which the world is made.

6

****

The ancient Milesian philosophers were not, after all,
simple-minded thinkers. Thales' views, based on observation and reflection, were a major advancement over
earlier superstitious, nonnatural accounts of the world.
Anaximander and Anaximenes introduced advances that
are now basic to science: explanation through a principle
of abstraction and quantitative explanation of qualitative
difference. The strides of the Milesians were great. We
would not have modern science without these ideas, and
few of us could have broken through the molds of the
mind to make such breakthroughs if we were in their
position.

7

Notes

[1]See Ring 20-21 and Lloyd 18-20. Ring and others believe Thales characterized all matter as forms of water. Lloyd and others believe Thales characterized only the origin of the universe when he claimed water as basic.

Works Cited

Allen, Reginald E. Greek Philosophy: Thales to Aristotle. New York: Free Press, 1966.

Cornford, F. M. From Religion to Philosophy. New York: Harper, 1957.

Diamandopoulos, P. "Anaximenes," Encyclopedia of Philosophy. 1967 ed.

Guthrie, W. K. C. The Greek Philosophers: From Thales to Aristotle. New York: Harper, 1950.

Guthrie, W. K. C. A History of Greek Philosophy. Vol. 1. Cambridge: Cambridge University Press, 1962.

Lloyd, G. E. R. Early Greek Science: Thales to Aristotle. New York: Norton, 1970.

8

Peters, F. E. Greek Philosophical Terms: A Historical
Lexicon. New York: New York University Press,
1967.

Ring, Merrill. Beginning with the Pre-Socratics. Mountain View, CA: Mayfield, 1987.

Bibliography

Anson, Chris M. and Lance E. Wilcox. *A Field Guide to Writing*. New York: HarperCollins, 1992.

Chicago Manual of Style. 13th ed. Chicago: University of Chicago Press, 1982.

Copperud, Roy H. *American Usage and Style: The Consensus*. New York: Van Nostrand Reinhold, 1979.

Durant, Will. *The Story of Philosophy*. New York: Washington Square Press, 1952.

Edwards, Paul, ed. *The Encyclopedia of Philosophy*. New York: Macmillan & Free Press, 1967.

Gibaldi, Joseph and Walter S. Achtert. *MLA Handbook for Writers of Research Papers*. New York: The Modern Language Association of America, 1988.

Hodges, John C., et al. *Harbrace College Handbook*. 11th ed. New York: Harcourt, 1990.

Jones, W. T. *A History of Western Philosophy*. 4 vol. New York: Harcourt, 1969.

Judd, Karen. *Copyediting: A Practical Guide*. 2nd ed. Los Altos, CA: Crisp, 1989.

Lester, James D. *Writing Research Papers: A Complete Guide*. 6th ed. New York: HarperCollins, 1990.

Lineback, Richard H., ed. *The Philosopher's Index.* Philosophy Documentation Center. Bowling Green, OH: Bowling Green University, 1967–1992.

Library of Congress Classification. Class B. Subclasses B–BJ, BL–BQ, BR–BV, BX. 4th ed. Washington, D.C.: Library of Congress, 1989.

Longyear, Marie, ed. *McGraw-Hill Style Manual: A Concise Guide for Writers and Editors.* New York: McGraw-Hill, 1983.

Matson, Wallace I. *A New History of Philosophy.* 2 vol. San Diego: Harcourt, 1987.

Meiland, Jack. *College Thinking: How to Get the Best Out of College.* New York: New American Library, 1981.

Osborn, Jeanne. *Dewey Decimal Classification, 19th Edition: A Study Manual.* Littleton, CO: Libraries Unlimited, 1982.

Peters, F. E. *Greek Philosophical Terms: A Historical Lexicon.* New York: New York University Press, 1967.

Philosophy Documentation Center catalog. Bowling Green, OH: Bowling Green State University, 1992.

Randall, John Herman, Jr. *The Career of Philosophy.* 2 vol. New York: Columbia University Press, 1965.

Readers' Guide to Periodical Literature. New York: H. W. Wilson, 1890–1992.

Roberts, Edgar V. *Writing Themes About Literature.* Englewood Cliffs, NJ: Prentice-Hall, 1964.

Rosen, Leonard J. and Laurence Behrens. *Writing Papers in College.* Boston: Little, Brown, 1986.

Rosnow, Ralph L. and Mimi Rosnow. *Writing Papers in Psychology.* Belmont, CA: Wadsworth, 1992.

Roth, Audrey J. *The Research Paper: Process, Form, and Content.* Belmont, CA: Wadsworth, 1989.

Russell, Bertrand. *A History of Western Philosophy.* New York: Simon & Schuster, 1945.

Seech, Zachary. *Logic in Everyday Life: Practical Reasoning Skills.* Belmont, CA: Wadsworth, 1988.

Seech, Zachary. *Open Minds and Everyday Reasoning.* Belmont, CA: Wadsworth, 1993.

Strunk, William, Jr. and E. B. White. *Elements of Style.* 3rd ed. New York: Macmillan, 1979.

Turabian, Kate L. *A Manual for Writers of Term Papers, Theses, and Dissertations.* Chicago: University of Chicago Press, 1973.

Turabian, Kate L. *Student's Guide for Writing College Papers.* Chicago: University of Chicago Press, 1976.

Woodhouse, Mark B. *A Preface to Philosophy.* Belmont, CA: Wadsworth, 1990.

Index